FEB 04

THE STORY OF THE
Fens

THE STORY OF THE
Fens

Valerie Gerrard

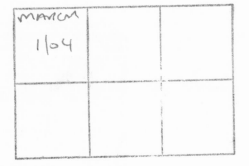

MARCM
1/04

ROBERT HALE · LONDON

© Valerie Gerrard 2003
First published in Great Britain 2003

ISBN 0 7090 7071 3

Robert Hale Limited
Clerkenwell House
Clerkenwell Green
London EC1R 0HT

A catalogue record for this book is available from the British Library

2 4 6 8 10 9 7 5 3 1

Typeset in 11/13½ Bitstream Arrus
Printed in Great Britain by
St Edmundsbury Press Limited
and bound by Woolnough Bookbinding Limited

Between pages 96 and 97

Between pages 128 and 129

Between pages 160 and 161

black and white

Picture Credits

Cambridgeshire Collection, Cambridgeshire Libraries: 7, 64–7. Welney Wildfowl and Wetlands Trust: 10, 11, 12, 48, 49, 56, 58, 59. Ely Museum: 14, 15, 16, 23, 30, 31, 32, 36. Julie Royle: 40. Heritage Museum: 50. The Environment Agency: 60–3, 68–71.

Acknowledgements

This book is the result of what may at first seem an unlikely fascination with the Fens. Unlikely, because I am not a native. I come from a land of massive mountains and sea – it is hard to imagine anywhere more different from the Fens than the west coast of British Columbia in Canada. Perhaps the only thing the two landscapes have in common is a sense of isolation, of being apart from the rest of the world.

I lived for several years in and around the Fens without making this connection. To me, as to many others new to the area, it was simply flat, fairly peaceful and full of farms. Then I found myself working for the Environment Agency, in the Flood Defence Department, and, as I learned the true story behind the long, straight rivers and the oddly raised fields, the fascination began. As I started to understand the on-going mechanism of the Ouse Washes and the constant vigilance that is required to keep the Fens under control, I was hooked. I determined to write the story of land drainage and flood defence in a way that was accessible to those not already experts on the subject.

Like so many bright ideas, this one lay dormant for several years, during which time I wrote several brochures for the Environment Agency and learned even more about the intricacies of drainage and defence. In the course of my work, I visited various sluices, stations and other sites and continued to marvel at the feats of engineering that have, over the centuries, resulted in the Fens we see today. I talked to many people about the possibility of this book, and all thought it a good idea, but still it remained just an idea. The missing link came from an unexpected source. One day, lying stretched out on a chiropractor's table, I once again outlined my ideas. As he realigned my spine, my chiropractor suggested that I write the *whole* story of the Fens – not just the drainage, but everything from early settlers to later invaders, and on up to the present day.

I embarked on the necessary research and immediately discovered that there was so much, much more to the Fens than I had ever imagined. It is extraordinary how much of England's history has taken place in this often overlooked area. I soon came to see the Fens as much more than an engineering marvel: it was a land with a long and complicated past.

Inevitably, I have drawn upon many sources for information and assistance, and would like to express my gratitude. All the books mentioned in the bibliography have been an enormous help; and there were many individuals and organizations who provided even more information, as well as stories and pictures. My thanks to: BBC Radio Cambridgeshire (and in particular Gerald Mains), Rameen Marinus Bierens, Arie De Vriet, the Cambridgeshire Collection, the Department of Trade and Industry, Ely Museum, the Environment Agency, Ian Hart, Heritage Hall Museum in Downham Market, The National Farmers' Union, Fenland District Council, Prickwillow Drainage Museum, Welney Wildfowl and Wetlands Trust, the Wisbech Museum, and many, many more. Special thanks to Carolyn Jones who provided line drawings, as well as enlisting and co-ordinating the help of two colleagues: Andrew Smee and Peter Marshall. Thank you all so much.

It doesn't end there. The Bridge Boatyard in Ely provided me with the means to explore the Fens from the River Ouse, in the form of a magnificent hire boat on which I spent a wonderful week taking photographs and soaking in the atmosphere. And I owe particular thanks to my son, James Gerrard, who so efficiently captained that expedition (even when my doubtful navigation skills grounded us in a backwater of the River Wissey one afternoon). My final thank you is to Jeff Gerrard who, in addition to providing the schematic layout and illustration, gave me more support than could reasonably be asked for and, quite literally, made the whole thing happen.

Chronology of the Fens in English History

Period/ monarch	England	The Fens

c. 500,000 BC–AD 43: Early Britain

	500,000–4500 BC: Paleolithic (Old Stone Age)	
	125,000 BC: Last Ice Age begins	
		c. 10,000 BC: Sea and river water flow into the area
	c. 25,000 BC: Ice Cap begins to retreat	
	c. 10,000 BC: Britain separates from Continent	
	c. 4000 BC: Immigrants arrive from Europe	
	c. 3200 BC: Stonehenge built	
		c. 2000 BC: Relatively dry period; some people move deeper into Fens
	c. 1900 BC: Beaker Culture arrives from Holland and the Rhineland	
	c. 800 BC: First Celtic invasion	
	700 BC: Iron Age begins	*700 BC*: Celts arrive
		600 BC: Wet period; people retreat to Fen edges and islands
	55 BC: Julius Caesar lands in Britain – has to retreat	
	54 BC: Caesar lands again – reaches Essex before retreating	

AD 43–410: Romans

	43: Roman invasion under Aulus Plautus	*43–*: Roman forts established in East Anglia
		47: Iceni defeated in East Anglia
		54–68: Romans build Carr Dyke, also many other canals, embankments and sea defences
		61–62: Boudicca's revolt
		end-3rd century: all traces of Romans gone
		410–: Fens revert to wilderness of floods and marshes

410–1066: Anglo-Saxons

	c. 406–: Anglo-Saxon invasions	Flood defences and drainage works continue deteriorating throughout the Anglo-Saxon period
		c. 600–: Hermit monks arrive in the Fens; begin to form brotherhoods
		c. 620–625: King Radwald of East Anglia buried at Sutton Hoo

c. 672: Etheldreda founds monastery at Ely
8th/9th centuries: Abbeys prosper
716: Building of Crowland Abbey begins

787: Viking invasions begin
793: First Viking raid – on Lindisfarne
802–839: Egbert, first King of the English

869: Danes occupy East Anglia and kill
(St) Edmund, King of East Anglia
870: Crowland, Peterborough and Ely abbeys
sacked by Vikings

c. 870: England divided into shires

871–899: Alfred the Great

871: 'Danelaw' ceded to the Danes

978–1010: Ethelred II ('the Unready')

1016–1035: Canute (Cnut)

c. 1020: King's Dyke built

1066: Harold II Godwinson

1066: Norman invasion; Harold killed at
Battle of Hastings

1066–1154: Normans

1066–1087: William I

1066: William builds castles at Ely and Wisbech
1070–1071: Rising led by Hereward the Wake –
suppressed

1087–1100: William II

1090: Building of Ely and Norwich cathedrals
begins

1100–1135: Henry I

1109: Henry appoints first Bishop of Ely

1135–1154: Stephen

1135: Bishop of Ely opposes King Stephen
1142: Stephen uses French troops to fight the
Barons at the Isle of Ely
1143–4: Geoffrey de Mandeville terrorizes the Fens

1154–1399: Plantagenets

1154–1189: Henry II

13th–15th centuries: Fens very wet again

1189–1199: Richard I (Lionheart)
1199–1216: John

1209: Cambridge University founded
1214–15: Fen Barons play major part in creating
Magna Carta
1216: King John loses royal treasure in the Wash;
dies days later

1215: Magna Carta

1216–1272: Henry III
1225: Law of Land

1258: First Commissioners of Sewers appointed
1260: Barons, at war with Crown, make a stand at
Ely; the King eventually prevails

1272–1307: **Edward I**

1307–1327: **Edward II**

1327–1377: **Edward III**
1337–1453: Hundred Years' War
c. 1345–1400: Geoffrey Chaucer
1348–c. 1440: Black Death

1377–1399: **Richard II**
1381: Poll tax introduced at 1 shilling per head; Peasants' Revolt ensues

1381: Peasants riot in Ely and Littleport

1399–1485: Lancaster and York

1399–1413: **Henry IV**

1400: Wisbech nearly destroyed by floods
c. 1400: Act of Parliament grants Commissioners of Sewers rights to collect taxes and punish tax evaders

1413–1422: **Henry V**
1415: Battle of Agincourt

1427: Commissioners of Sewers given extra powers

1422–1461: **Henry VI**
1455–85: Wars of the Roses

1461–1483: **Edward IV**
1475: William Caxton produces first printed books in English

1483: **Edward V**

1483–1485: **Richard III**

1485–1603: Tudors

1485–1509: **Henry VII**
1492: Columbus discovers the New World

1500s: Neglect of drainage system leads to years of flooding

1509–1547: **Henry VIII**
1536, 1539: Dissolution of the monasteries

1536: Catherine of Aragon dies at Kimbolton

1547–1553: **Edward VI**

1553–1558: **Mary**

1558–1603: **Elizabeth I**
1564–1616: Shakespeare's lifetime

1570: High tides break the Roman bank between Wisbech and Walsoken; floods reach inland as far as Bedford

1577–80: Drake circumnavigates the world

1587: Mary, Queen of Scots, buried at Peterborough (removed to Westminster Abbey 1612)
1599: Oliver Cromwell born in Huntingdon

13

1603–1714: Stuarts

1603–1625: James I

> 1605: Gunpowder Plot

> 1618–48: Thirty Years' War
> 1620: Pilgrim Fathers sail for America

1625–1649: Charles I

> 1642–8: Civil War
> 1649: Charles I executed; Oliver Cromwell
>   declares Commonwealth

[1649–1660: Commonwealth and Protectorate]

> 1653–8: Cromwell is Lord Protector
> 1660: Restoration of the monarchy

1660–1685: Charles II

> 1664–5: Great Plague
> 1665–7: Second Anglo-Dutch War
> 1666: Great Fire of London

1685–1688: James II

1689–1702: William and Mary

1702–1714: Anne

1600–30: Almost constant flooding
1605: Popham's Eau cut, draining the area
  around Upware

1621: Cornelius Vermuyden arrives in
  England

early 17th century: Charles I plans to build royal
  estate at Manea
1629: Vermuyden knighted
c. 1630: Gentlemen Adventurers formed
1637: Fen drainage declared 'complete'

1652: Fen drainage 'completed' for the second time

1667: Vermuyden dies in obscurity in London
late 17th century: Peat shrinkage causes severe
  flooding
late 17th to 18th centuries: Windmills used to drain
  Fens

1713: Denver Sluice collapses

1714–1901: Hanoverians

1714–1727: George I

1727–1760: George II

> 1751: New Year's Day moved back from
>   2 March to 1 January
> 1756–63: Seven Years' War

1760–1820: George III

> 1775: James Watt perfects steam engine
> late 18th century: Bread riots
> 1802: Factory Acts
> 1805: Battle of Trafalgar
> 1807: Abolition of slavery
> 1815: Battle of Waterloo

1820–1830: George IV (Regent 1811–1820)

1830–1837: William IV

c. 1700s–1750s: Land continues to shrink;
  flooding gets worse

1763: First speed skating match held on Fens

1816: Littleport Riots

1820: Steam-driven pumps introduced to the Fens

14

1837–1901: Victoria

1838–51: Robert Owen forms workers'
co-operative at Manea
1840: More protests against poverty and
mechanization: 'Captain Swing'

1844, 1847: Factory Acts
1851: The Great Exhibition

1851: Whittlesey Mere drained
1852: Holme Fen Post sunk

1853–6: Crimean War
1884: Third Reform Act: agricultural workers
given the vote

1901–: Saxe-Coburg-Gotha (from 1917, Windsor)

1901–1910: Edward VII

1910–1936: George V

Fens now a key agricultural area

1914–18: World War I
1926: General Strike
1928: Women get the vote at 21
1929–35: Great Depression

1930s–1940s: Diesel pumps used to drain Fens
1930–54: £10 million spent on raising and
strengthening river banks

1936: Edward VIII

1936–1952: George VI

1936, 1937, 1939: Major flooding

1939–45: World War II
1947: Fuel crisis (coal shortage)

1947: Biggest flood for over a century. Last
significant steam pump (Streatham Steam
Pump) closed
1950–: Electric pumps used to drain the Fens

1952–: Elizabeth II

1953: Major flooding: lives lost
1954–64: Great Ouse Protection Scheme
implemented – the largest drainage project
since the 17th century

1973: Britain joins EEC
1979–1990: Margaret Thatcher is Britain's
first woman Prime Minister

1980s: Extensive refurbishment of Denver Sluice

1982: Falklands War

1990s: Ouse Washes Flood Control Strategy
implemented at a cost of £8 million

1991: Gulf War

1994: Channel Tunnel opens
1997: Labour wins General Election after
18 years of Conservative rule
2001: £400m spent on flood defence

1998: Land levels have dropped by up to 20 metres
from seventeenth-century pre-drainage levels
1998–2003: Major flooding
2001: DEFRA earmarks £30m for improving sea
defences in Norfolk
2002: Both pumps at newly improved Welches
Dam pumping station fail simultaneously

Introduction

History isn't just the story of the past; in many ways it is a frame for the present and a window on the future. The East Anglian Fens are full of fascination both in the past and the present. Over the years, writers such as Charles Kingsley and Daniel Defoe have described the area. In his 1906 book of essays *Hills and the Sea*, Hilaire Belloc, an author less often associated with the Fens, was struck by the unique qualities of the land: 'Upon the very limit of the Fens, not a hundred feet in height, but very sharp against the level, there is a lonely little hill. From the edge of that hill the land seems very vague; the flat line of the horizon is the only boundary, and that horizon mixes into watery clouds. ... Great catastrophes have certainly overcome this countryside ... it is probable that, coincidentally with every grave lesion in the continuity of our civilization, the Fens suffered, for they always needed the perpetual attention of man to keep them fully inhabited and cultured. Nowhere that I have been to in the world does the land fade into the sea so inconspicuously.' Those familiar with the Fens' story will immediately understand the fascination, but many will look over an uninspiring bit of agricultural England and wonder what interest it could possibly hold.

A lot has happened in this unprepossessing land over the centuries. The first century AD saw the famous revolt of Boudicca, the fiery and by all accounts fearsome Iceni queen who led the Celts in a last desperate rebellion against the Roman conquerors. They wreaked havoc, burning Roman settlements and garrisons and killing hosts of Imperial soldiers before their final defeat signalled the end of British resistance against Roman rule. The eighth and ninth centuries saw the Viking Invasions, and the monasteries of the Fens were a very great part of what tempted the marauders across the Channel to loot and pillage. They made their way up

16

Fenland rivers to steal gold, silver, jewels and gems from the wealthy abbeys. For years they ravaged the Fens and East Anglia, before they settled on the lands they had terrorized and became Kings of England.

Familiar to many is the story of Hereward the Wake, the Lincolnshire landowner who headed the last stand of the English against the Normans. It all culminated in the Fen city of Ely in 1070. Although Hereward eventually failed, his exploits have become a part of English history. Then, in the thirteenth century, many of the Barons who forced King John to sign the Magna Carta, thus heralding the beginning of British democracy, were from Fenland, and they met and conspired in and around the Fens. There is also the Cromwell connection. The future Lord Protector was born just on the edge of the Fens in Huntingdon in 1599. He owned large estates throughout Fenland and lived for many years in Ely.

However, perhaps the most extraordinary thing about the Fens is that, although they now provide a good percentage of England's crops, they shouldn't be arable at all – or only barely. Before the seventeenth century, Fenland was true to its name: 'fen – a low marshy land often, or partially, covered with water: a morass or bog'. Much of the area was waterlogged and completely unsuitable for growing crops. Defoe described the area as 'the sink of no less than 13 counties', and indeed the low-lying Fen rivers are the drains for 6,000 square miles of land surrounding them. So it's not surprising that the rivers frequently overflowed their banks, flooding the surrounding area. Life here was hard. For much of the year, vast areas were under water, perhaps providing some grazing land for a few short weeks during the summer. The only places where any real cultivation could be confidently attempted were on areas of slightly higher ground, such as Ely and Ramsey, which were known as islands (the -ey or -y suffix comes from the Old English eg: land wholly or partly surrounded by water).

All this changed in the seventeenth century, when a massive project was undertaken to drain the Fens and make use of the good, rich soil that lay under water most of the time. That project had its pros and cons, but the result is undeniable: man changed the land. The Fens are no longer natural (and literal) fens. They are entirely man-made and continue to exist only through constant mainte-nance and vigilance.

The fens may now look like miles and miles of boring, flat fields, interrupted only by gently flowing rivers that seem to go on forever. But this is a façade. Those fields shouldn't be there. The rivers may flow gently now, but only thanks to the expenditure of millions of pounds and even more man-hours; those rivers have to be cleared and scoured and their waters pumped, diverted and stored in order to maintain that peaceful scene. The alternative is flooding – worse and worse flooding and eventual reversion to the 'morass or bog' of the original fenland. The constant effort that goes into keeping the Fens as they are today is astounding: millions of pounds each year, millions of man-hours – and it must not stop. The Fens may no longer be a swamp, but they are still subject to floods, and always will be. Man must work relentlessly to minimize the damage.

And what has all this created? An upside-down world, where the rivers are several feet higher than the surrounding fields they are meant to drain. How did that happen? It was an unexpected result of draining the land to turn it into an agricultural goldmine. The plan was flawed, but it is not a flaw which can be rectified – only controlled.

In the end, it is people rather than events that shape history. The spirit of the early settlers, the Breedlings and the Fen Tigers, colours the entire story of the Fens. These were a strange people who kept themselves very much to themselves – more than that: they hated 'foreigners', i.e. anyone who did not live in their waterlogged land. Their extraordinary lives were dependent on the soggy marshes, on which only they knew how to survive. This they did amazingly well, despite floods, incapacitating rheumatism and the ever-present 'Fen ague' (malaria), and their isolationism prevented, or at least slowed, change on the Fens for centuries. The fierce chauvinism has finally given way to the modern world, but the stubbornness remains. It can be seen in the way modern Fen dwellers refuse to give in to the inevitable floods, fighting them with as much determination as their ancestors ever did.

And the future? No one can predict that, but there is one undeniable fact. Either Man continues to maintain, at great cost, his creation that today we call Fenland, or Nature will have her way. The system of sluices, pumps, drains and embankments must be kept viable. There is no other option: constant control or the true fen returns. Centuries of work could be undone in a very few years.

1. A Land Out of Time

A great many descriptive names have been applied to the Fen Country. Perhaps the most common is the Drowned Lands: a reference to the constant flooding. Others, such as Britain's Breadbasket, seem directly contradictory. The Fens have sometimes been called The Land of Goshen (a happy place of light and plenty); but they have also been known as The Great Eastern Swamp.

Yet another name has been The Holy Land of the English – referring to a long period in the middle ages when Fenland monasteries and abbeys were influential. Then, there's Cromwell Country, a designation that obviously alludes to it being the birthplace of the man himself as well as to the Fen Country's role in the Civil War.

The variety and contradictions of these names show that the history of the Fens is a mosaic. Some of its pieces are large, spanning years or even centuries, others are tiny but very bright and play a major part in the tale. Looking at the whole mosaic and how its various parts combine and interact brings understanding of the Fens, their richness and significance.

So many elements make up this story, but the underlying theme is water and flood and land drainage – man's unchanging and yet ever-changing battle to tame the Fens, and to make the area habitable, hospitable and profitable. Why should Man want to go to such great effort and expense to drain this land? The answer lies in yet another name for the Fens: the Summer Lands. It was obvious that the area had great potential for farming if only the waters could be kept at bay. During the brief summer months, cattle could graze on rich grasses, and crops grew abundantly in the fertile soil. The problem was that the whole lot was likely to be washed away by the regular autumn and winter flooding. But the potential was there, and the Romans recognized it. They were probably the first to try to keep the land dry with embankments and drains. Others

21

followed suit, rerouting rivers and building more defences, but it wasn't until the seventeenth century that major and long-lasting changes were made – and these did not come without their fair share of setbacks and problems.

Of course, an important part of the tale is the lives of the people who lived on the Fens – from early European immigrants *c.* 4000 BC, to Celts, to Anglo-Saxons, and through to the modern men of the Fens. Fenlanders have always had an unusual tenacity and determination to endure in their strange and often unfriendly land, to survive it and make it work for them, rather than against them.

The following is a brief overview of the history of the Fens, from prehistory through to the present, intended to show how all the different parts, some of which span centuries, create the whole. Subsequent chapters will look at important elements in greater detail, and the chronological overview on pages 11 to 15 helps to put everything in place, both the course of Fenland history, and that of the rest of Britain.

Early Britain – c. 500,000 BC to AD 43

The first part of the story has nothing to do with the Fens, for 500,000 years ago they didn't exist. Nor, for that matter, did Britain, which was still connected to what is today Europe. In about 125,000 BC the last Ice Age began, and it was over a hundred thousand years before the ice cap began to retreat; Britain still did not exist as a separate land mass, and the Great Ouse was simply a small tributary of the Rhine. Around 10,000 BC Britain separated from the Continent, and it was at this time that rising sea levels began to fill the hollow of the Fen basin, created earlier by the retreating ice.

Some two thousand years after that some immigrants from Europe arrived, and a few of these may have settled on what would become the Fens. Certainly, the area was very accessible from Europe, and among later incomers were the Beaker Folk, who crossed from Holland. They were mainly agriculturalists, so would probably only have been interested in the higher lands. It is possible that, even at this early stage, man started to change the land he lived on, for there is evidence to suggest that areas may have been deliberately burned to create clearings to grow crops in – what today we call 'slash-and-burn' cultivation. Civilization began to take shape. Just outside the Fens, at the spot now known as Grime's

Graves in Norfolk, the site of an early flint mine provides evidence of industry on a fairly big scale. Some of the mine shafts were over 10 metres (32 feet) deep, and it is likely that the excavated flint was not only used locally, but was traded for other commodities from further afield.

The first Celtic immigrants appeared *c.* 800 BC, and these Iron-Age Europeans gradually spread through much of Britain, before the Romans eventually pushed most of them into Ireland, Wales and Scotland. By about 5000 BC the Fens were covered by a vast forest that lasted for some thousands of years. This explains the bog oaks: the preserved trunks of ancient trees that turn up all over the Fens, causing farmers to break their ploughs on the hard preserved wood buried in the soil. (The wood will not burn satis-factorily; recently, local artists have begun to carve bowls, etc. out of it, but there is no other practical use for these relics.) Some of the trees are huge. One found in the peat at Queen Adelaide Bridge in Ely in 1960 was 21 metres (70 feet) long. It was radiocarbon dated to 2535 BC ± 120 years. Another found at Stretham was 82 feet long and weighed eight tons. Not all, in fact, are oaks – some are hazel, others fir or yew. But all lie facing the same direction, with their tops pointing north-east.

The fact that the trunks are so long and lack lower branches indi-cates that they were part of a tall, dense forest and needed to grow very high to reach the sunlight – their lower parts would never see sufficient light to grow branches. But why did they fall? And why did they all fall in the same direction? The most commonly accepted theory is that over the years the trees were 'choked'. As decaying vegetation produced more and more peat, which became increasingly deep and damp, it became harder for the sap in the trees to rise; eventually the sap stopped altogether, and the trees began to rot. The suggestion is that, after a period of rotting, a particularly strong south-westerly gale blew them all down.

Flag Fen

The most important Bronze Age site in Europe is located on the fen edge, on the outskirts of modern Peterborough. The site at Flag Fen was discovered in 1982, during construction of a drainage ditch, and the timbers found were radiocarbon dated to 1000 BC. This discovery sparked a major archaeological project that has unearthed Bronze and Iron Age artefacts and a magnificent collec-

23

tion of pre-Roman metalwork – certainly one of the most extensive in Britain.

Flag Fen itself is a basin surrounded by slightly higher ground. In prehistoric times this higher ground was not flooded, and it was there that folk had their farms and houses. The lower land was usually under water during the winter, but was used during the summer to graze sheep and cattle.

Rising water levels made this bit of land attractive to people living elsewhere on the Fens, where floods were becoming more and more common. As a result, those living around Flag Fen decided they needed to protect their asset and built a 1-kilometre wall of posts across the access to the flood meadows. Hundreds of thousands of timbers were used. A huge platform of timber, supported by posts, was erected where the wall crossed a large area of open water. From this vantage point the inhabitants could defend their fen 'island'. There is no doubt that it was an impressive feat of engineering that allowed the folk of Flag Fen to retain ownership of the valuable summer grazing land for centuries.

The palisade was maintained for some 400 years but, even after it was abandoned around 950 BC, the site retained a religious significance. It is probable that the area was considered sacred. There are two possible reasons for that. First of all, the elevated land protected by the timber wall had provided sustenance for a very long time and no doubt contributed greatly to the well-being of those people. Additionally, great importance was placed on sacrifice, tribute and the powers of water. The site was surrounded by deep water, and it is likely that offerings were made to the gods who were believed to dwell therein. Items of great value would have been ceremoniously cast into the depths. Many objects, such as swords, ornaments and jewellery have been excavated. Sacrifices were made by ritually killing animals such as sheep and cattle and throwing them to the gods of the water. It is possible that some sacrifices were human, as bones of both humans and animals have been found. These relics date mainly from the Bronze Age, although the latest are from the early Iron Age. A Bronze Age and an Iron Age roundhouse have been reconstructed on the site, using information gleaned from the archaeological findings.

The historical importance of Flag Fen continues through to the Roman period, as the Fen Causeway road runs through the site, and a section of it can be clearly seen. There is also a medieval waterway, the Mustdyke, which would have been used for drainage and irrigation purposes.

The Romans – AD 43–410

Julius Caesar raided England in 55 and 54 BC, but both times was forced to retreat. However, when the Romans mounted a serious invasion in AD 43 they were successful, and they soon had forts and towns established all over England. Some of these were on the Fen edge, such as Peterborough and Godmanchester.

Queen Boudicca's famous revolt against the Romans took place in and around the Fens. Boudicca's Iceni were a Celtic tribe living in what is now Norfolk and Suffolk; men of the Gyrwe or Girvii tribe of the Fens joined the revolt in 61–62, but failed to best the Roman conquerors.

The Romans were the first to make any significant attempt to drain the Fens. Carr Dyke was excavated during the early years of occupation; it was mainly for navigational purposes, but may have had a drainage function. Certainly the Romans erected embankments to keep both fresh and sea water off the agricultural land, and they maintained them throughout their occupation. However, after the last Roman legion left Britain in 406, they soon deteriorated through neglect; much like the great Roman roads, these structures quickly disappeared, and all benefits were lost.

The Anglo-Saxons – AD 440–1066

Before the end of the fifth century the Fens had reverted to a wilderness of floods and marshes. The Anglo-Saxon invasions had begun even before the Romans left, and the Fens were closely involved. Indeed, many Anglo-Saxons settled in the area, which was part of what became known as East Anglia (originally the Kingdom of the East Angles).

Throughout the Anglo-Saxon period Fenland was suffering one of its periodic inundated phases. Truly the Great Eastern Swamp, the land supported little in the way of proper agriculture, and the Fenmen survived only through their stubbornness and determination not to be defeated. Those living on the edges of the swamps could grow crops on higher ground and, at least in the summer months, graze cattle on the marshes, as could those who inhabited

25

the Fen 'islands', such as Ely and Ramsey. But the vast majority of Fen folk lived harsh, short lives, eking out a marginal, almost amphibious, existence. The ever-present waters provided food and livelihood: they caught fish and eels in the rivers, shot or trapped wildfowl in the swamps, and harvested the marsh grasses and reeds to use as building materials. In many respects, England's succession of invaders had little impact on the people who lived deep in the Fens. Their waterlogged lands were of no interest to the invaders, and the Fen folk were far too preoccupied with their constant battle against the Fens to pay the newcomers much attention. Indeed, they were a particularly insular people, very suspicious of 'foreigners'.

Cambridge camels. Crossing the swamps on stilts was a
common solution to getting around in the wet season.

It was during this period that the story of the Church in the Fens begins. In the seventh century an abbey was built in Crowland in memory of St Guthlac, a hermit who had seen the Fens as somewhere to escape the temptations of life and dedicate his existence to God. By the 700s and 800s, there were several abbeys in the Fens and they were thriving, owning more and more of the land and, incidentally, making a great profit from the eel trade. But such prosperity attracted a new wave of invaders, who used the waters of the Fens as a handy ingress to the rest of England: the Vikings. By 869, after less than a hundred years, the Danes had occupied all of East Anglia, which eventually formed part of the Danelaw, the area north-east of Watling Street that King Alfred ceded to the Danes in 878, and which his grandsons reconquered by 955.

The Normans – AD 1066–1154

As is well known, William I defeated King Harold II at the Battle of Hastings in 1066, and this was the start of Norman occupation. The Normans' conquest of England was not an easy one, however, and one of the best known attempts to stave them off was staged by Hereward the Wake. The Normans tried to cross the treacherous Fens to attack Ely by building a sort of pontoon bridge across the swamps. Having a much better understanding of the marshes than the attackers, Hereward and his supporters hid among the long reeds and set them on fire. Thousands of invading soldiers died, either roasted in their armour or drowned in the bogs into which they desperately jumped. Unfortunately, Hereward's victory was short-lived as a year later, in 1071, he and his cause were betrayed by some of the monks at Ely, and the last stand against the Norman invaders ended in defeat.

The influence of the Church grew during this period, with the construction of both Ely and Norwich cathedrals beginning in 1090, and in 1109 Henry I appointed the first Bishop of Ely.

The Plantagenets – AD 1154–1399

By the beginning of the thirteenth century, the Fens had entered another soggy part of the cycle. Frequent flooding and constant wet conditions made the area a very unpleasant place. There is evidence of local landowners' concern, and the first Commissioners of Sewers were appointed in 1258 in an attempt to exert some central control over the problem.

Fen barons and landowners had also played a significant part in a pivotal piece of English history at the beginning of the century. Many of the barons who rebelled against King John and eventually forced him to sign the Magna Carta in 1215 were Fen landowners. Indeed, the first draft of this famous document, which laid the foundation for democracy in England, was initially presented to Fen lords and others at a secret meeting in Bury St Edmunds, just outside the edge of the Fens.

Lancaster and York

The Commissioners of Sewers found it hard going building and maintaining any kind of drainage system. The biggest problem was encouraging the people to pay for the work. In approximately 1400 the Commissioners were given the right to collect taxes and punish those who would not pay.

Between 1487 and 1490 John Morton, Bishop of Ely (and later Archbishop of Canterbury) undertook work to straighten the River Nene in an attempt to alleviate terrible silting problems in Wisbech which at that time lay on the coast, and was a port with a great deal of trade. After completing Morton's Leam, he had grand plans for further drainage works, but these were thwarted by the Wars of the Roses.

The Tudors – AD 1485–1603

The Dissolution of the Monasteries in 1536 and 1539 had a major and catastrophic effect on the Fens. The monastic institutions had become major landowners in the Fens and, as such, initiated and supervised most of the land drainage work. When they fell, no one bothered to maintain the flood defences. Instead of one landlord, the Church, there were now hundreds of landowners, with neither the organization nor the resources to maintain outfalls, drains and embankments.

In 1570 unusually high tides broke through the old Roman sea defences, resulting in major floods as far inland as Bedfordshire.

The Stuarts – AD 1603–1714

This was a key period in the history of the Fens for two reasons. One major influence was the Civil War. Oliver Cromwell was born in Huntingdon, just outside the Fen edge, and lived later in St Ives and then Ely. Many of his soldiers were Fen-dwellers, and there is no doubt that the Civil War had an enormous effect on those living in the area.

However, by far the greatest event of this period and, in terms of drainage and flood defence, the most significant event so far on the Fens, came about in 1630 when King Charles I instructed the Earl of Bedford to set about draining the Fens properly. The Earl put together a band of fellow nobles, who called themselves The Adventurers, to fund and oversee the work, and a Dutchman, Cornelius Vermuyden, was commissioned to carry it out. Vermuyden made great changes to the Fen landscape – rivers were straightened and rerouted and new rivers dug out by hand – and this was the beginning of the Fen country we know today. It should be noted, however, that the scheme was far from a success initially, and by the end of this period the Fens were once again plagued by constant flooding. Much remained to be done before Vermuyden's scheme could be even partially successful.

The Hanoverians – AD 1714–1901

For a time, windmills, or wind-engines, were employed in great numbers all across the Fens to try to solve the drainage problems. The basic flaw in Vermuyden's scheme was that the newly drained land was composed largely of porous peat, and this was shrinking as the water was drained off it. Water cannot run uphill, and soon the rivers, whose beds consisted of harder sand and gravel, were running above the level of the surrounding land, resulting in devastating flooding. Vermuyden had caused embankments to be built alongside the rivers, but these were insufficient to contain the waters at all times. The windmills were used to try to defy gravity and pump the water off the fields and up into the rivers. Although better than nothing, they were wind-dependent and not really equal to the mammoth task. Frequent flooding continued to wreak havoc.

Then came the next great revolution – the age of steam. By 1820 steam-driven engines had arrived on the Fens, and they made an enormous difference. No longer dependent on wind and weather conditions, they enabled farmers and landowners to get the waters off their soggy fields and into the rivers, which would take them to the sea.

The nineteenth-century agricultural depression was a period of social upheaval all across England, and the Fens saw their share. The price of grain rose steeply, so that many could no longer afford a loaf of bread. As bread was the staple diet of many a labourer and his family, the situation soon became intolerable. In 1816 farm labourers from the Littleport area decided to take the matter into their own hands. Sixty men, including some who had recently returned from the Napoleonic Wars only to find themselves unable to feed their families, confronted local gentry demanding fair wages and food. The frightened landowers initially agreed to their demands, but they were really only buying time. The angry workers marched to Ely, and there things got completely out of hand, resulting in looting and fighting. Soldiers were sent in to stop the riot, and almost one hundred protesters were rounded up and tried. Most were jailed or deported to the penal colony of Botany Bay in Australia; five were hanged. More protests occurred, particularly in the 1840s, but the hungry workers were treated harshly and never gained the upper hand.

The social revolution continued. The Factory Acts of 1844 and 1847 had little effect on the people of the Fens. It could be argued that the Third Reform Act of 1884, giving agricultural workers the vote, was more significant for Fen folk but, for the most part, they were continuing as they had always done – working long, hard days making the most of the land. Flooding was now better controlled than it had ever been, but it remained a constant threat nonetheless.

In 1851, the last remaining mere on the Fens, Whittlesey Mere, was drained. The Fens would now be recognizable to a twenty-first-century visitor, with acres of arable land lying underneath the ever dominant Fen sky. That's another name for the Fens: Land of the Three-quarter Sky. By now, this is certainly what it had become.

Saxe-Goburg-Gotha/Windsor – AD 1901–

Both the First and Second World Wars had a significant effect on the Fens. The area's importance for food-growing was recognized, and resources were put into increasing its reliability through drainage, flood defence and maintenance. Nevertheless, the cyclical nature of the Fens is not to be denied, and 1936, 1937 and 1939 saw more major flooding.

But it was not just as Britain's Breadbasket that the Fens played a major part in World War II. Air force bases were dotted in and around the Fens, and the famous Pathfinders were frequently seen in the Fen skies, taking off from nearby bases. And the relationship between the US and the Fens, established then, continues to this day, for there is still a US Air Force presence in the area.

During the 1930s and 1940s steam-driven drainage pumps gave way to diesel, and this increased efficiency even further. Nevertheless, constant vigilance was still essential, as became apparent when the worst flooding event in memory took everyone by surprise in 1947. Within days, a freak combination of weather conditions saw nearly 25 square kilometres (10 square miles) of the Fens under water. The flood lasted for two weeks, and miraculously no lives were lost, but the cost in livestock, property and security was immense.

After that, the waters of the Fens were quiescent for a while. Major drainage works were undertaken, including the Great Ouse Protection Scheme (this project, which cost more than £10 million in the 1950s, was far and away the biggest drainage scheme attempted since Vermuyden's efforts in the 1600s). Further extensive works followed, but in 1998 the cycle started again, and there have been major floods each year since then.

The Fens seem always to have lagged behind the rest of the country in progress and innovation. No doubt the centuries-long struggle simply to survive in the lonely marshes had a great deal to do with that. But all has changed now. Farms are cultivated using the latest technology, and modern towns and cities exist where the ancient Fenmen used to fish, trap eels and shoot wildfowl. And it is not just farming technology that has come to the area. Right on the very edge of the Fens, around Cambridge, is one of Britain's most important and prestigious centres of innovation – Silicone Fen, home to hundreds of IT and high-tech companies of international importance.

Yet, in a way, despite modern communication and transportation, Fenland still seems a world apart. Perhaps it is the ever-independent spirit of Fenlanders that keeps it a land different from any other. Admittedly, the area we call the Fens is no longer true fens at all – there are still floods, and the need for constant vigilance, but the Drowned Lands, the Great Eastern Swamp, no longer exist. All the same, something lingers on, enhanced perhaps by the loneliness of the land, the vast bleak stretches of flat ground under an enormous and ever-changing sky. Walking along an unnaturally straight river, following its purposeful path to the sea, it is not difficult to imagine mad monks, crazed with malaria, making their

31

homes in the reeds, or Viking ships making their way inexorably upstream. A Breedling, an ancient Fenman, would not look out of place, stalking through the reeds on his stilts.

Perhaps what makes the Fens different is that history has not shaped this land – the land itself has shaped its own history.

The River Great Ouse near Ely

Reed beds provided the fenmen with building materials for centuries

Changing ground level of the Fens illustrated by post at Flag Fen

Among the ruins of Crowland Abbey. The headless statues are probably victims of the dissolution of the monasteries

Reconstruction of Bronze Age round house at Flag Fen

Remains of Bronze Age wall designed to protect land at Flag Fen

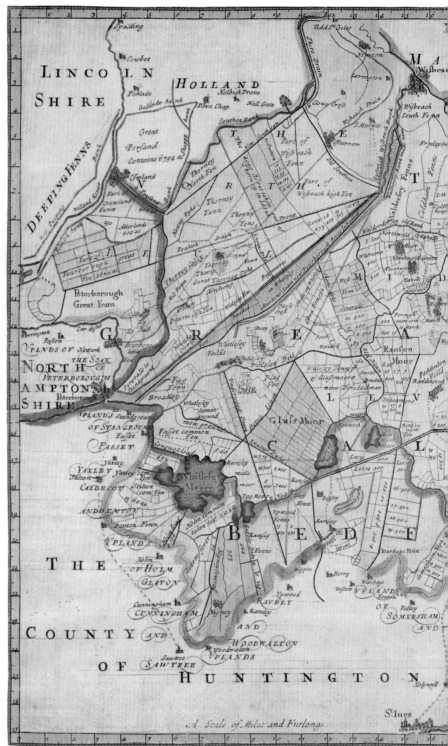

Published by Cambridgeshire Libraries from copy in the Library collection. Printed by Black Bear Press Limited, Cambridge. 1992.

A

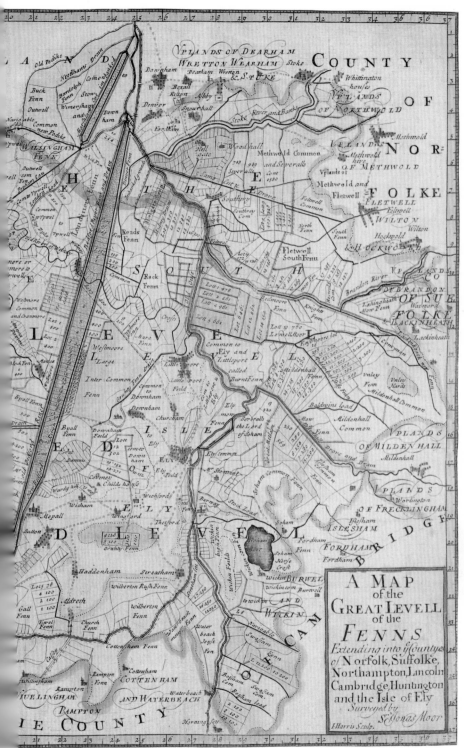

A MAP of the GREAT LEVELL of the FENNS Extending into y^e Countyes of Norfolk, Suffolke, Northampton, Lincoln Cambridge, Huntington and the Isle of Ely Surveyed by Sr Jonas Moor

Harris Sculp.

Cambridgeshire Map—No. 5. J. Moore—A map of the great levell of the Fenns 1684(1720)

ens

Archaeological excavation continues at Flag Fen, as more Iron Age and Bronze Age artefacts are discovered

The Great River Ouse, near the Cutter Inn at Ely

Miles and miles of flat fields near Welney

Flood at Welney

The Washes in flood near Welney in the 1990s

Denver Complex from the south, showing sluices and navigation lock

2. Drownings

Throughout history the Fens have seen invaders come and go and wars won and lost. There has been social unrest, riots and even revolution. But one thing has remained constant – one repeating cycle has shaped the pattern of life in the Fens over centuries: floods. And not merely floods but inundations – constant 'drownings' – are a key element in the tale.

As we have seen, the Fens did not exist before the end of the last Ice Age when retreating glaciers gouged out a hollow in East Anglia. Approximately 12,000 years ago, as Britain split off from the Continent, the rising waters of the Wash poured down into it from the north. At the same time, rivers flowing from the south deposited quantities of sand and silt in the hollow, creating the Fen basin.

However, the Fens as they are known today were yet to come: the area was blanketed with woods – oak, yew and pine all thrived. The next 4000 years saw periodic inundation by rising sea levels and flooding rivers, so that by about 4000 BC the swamps made their first appearance. The great forests had fallen to the waters, and a land of swamps, mudflats and lagoons was often washed over by the sea.

Now begins the unending climatic cycle so familiar in the Fens: relatively dry periods interspersed with dreary, wet and soggy periods featuring dramatic and devastating floods. The Fens first became habitable when the salt waters receded around 3000 BC. But a thousand years later, at the start of the Bronze Age, cooler and wetter conditions returned. Grazings were waterlogged and paths impassable. This was when man began his battle against the floods, building trackways across the drowned swamps. As the Bronze Age progressed, the pattern changed again. Like most of the rest of Britain, the Fens enjoyed warmer and drier weather, and the early dwellers began to make their homes and livings deeper and deeper in the Fens. Then around 600 BC, as the Bronze Age gave way to the Iron Age, the waters returned; fields became marshes, and the inhabitants retreated to fen edges and islands.

The cycle of inundation was now firmly established. The Fens had become 'Summer Lands', as they were to be known in later years, where limited cultivation and grazing was possible for just a few months in summer. Only a handful of isolated patches of higher land remained dry enough to sustain any kind of year-round agriculture; these were the fen islands.

But still the landscape was not as it is today. Although the great forests had fallen to rivers and tide, in Roman times the area was still fairly well forested with oak, ash and pine, and the Romans tried to bring some order to the drowned lands. They raised river and sea banks, built canals and maintained outfalls. Man was making his first significant attempts to tame the Fens, apparently successfully. However, after the Romans left in AD 410, a key factor in the struggle to control the Fens became apparent. Like so much that the Romans left behind, their sea defences were neglected and fell into disrepair; banks and dykes eroded, letting the salt water back on to the land. Outfalls became clogged with silt, and the water couldn't get away to the sea. Reinforced river banks gave way, spilling water out on to the fields. The Fens were drowned once more.

In the Anglo-Saxon era vast areas were uninhabitable. Any people who managed to survive the constant flooding and consequent destruction, disease and death lived once more on the islands. In the 600s the hermit St Guthlac saw a hostile land of 'vast marshes, with here a black pool of waters, now foul running streams, also many islands, reeds, hillocks and thickets', and the Fens remained in this soggy state for many years, the inhabitants surviving by exploiting the few resources these waterlogged lands could provide – reeds, fish, wildfowl and eels.

It wasn't until the thirteenth century that further attempts were made to tame the land. By then the Church was a major landowner in the Fens, and the Benedictine monks at Thorney Abbey (itself on a fen island) drained part of their estate and created, at least in that area, a pleasant land that the inhabitants of a few centuries before would not have recognized. Indeed, in the twelfth century, William of Malmesbury described the Fens as 'a very paradise ... a heaven for the delight and beauty thereof'. It is more likely, though, that this great improvement was the result of the cyclical pattern of flooding on the Fens, rather than the fruit of the monks' work – less than two decades later the floods came again, and in pretty dramatic fashion. In 1215 King John was travelling from King's Lynn to Lincoln with his retinue, including a baggage train that contained silver and gold drinking vessels and the King's personal collection of gems. In what can only be assumed to be an unexpected fashion, the Fens reverted to form. A contemporary report states: 'The ground opened in the midst of the waters, and whirlpools sucked in everything, men and horses.' John could only watch as the royal escort and the Plantagenet regalia disappeared into the Wash. (The treasure has never been found, despite numerous attempts over the years.)

During the course of the thirteenth century the situation deteriorated. Exceptionally high tides in 1236 and 1260 drowned hundreds of people. A dead whale was washed up on the shore at Wisbech, and the town itself was nearly destroyed by floods. Indeed flooding continued to be a way of life for centuries. Of course, there were a few dry years but from the thirteenth to the fifteenth centuries fields were generally drowned for most of the year. The sixteenth century, too, saw many floods all across the Fens. Wisbech and numerous marshland villages were inundated with waters from both rivers and sea year after sodden year. In 1570 the old Roman bank between Wisbech and Walsoken burst; villages, farms and fields that were not normally at risk were affected, and flooding reached inland as far as Bedfordshire. In the Cambridgeshire village of Over, a contemporary reports, 'in one moiste summer and an hard wynter following, they loste more by death and drowning of cattell than they gained by the fennes in three years' – and this was the picture all across the Fens, as high tides and horrendous rainfall caused rivers to burst their banks and cover houses and fields. At one point in the late 1500s a sailing boat was deposited on the roof of a house several miles inland. An Elizabethan survey of Thorney noted '16,000 acres of fen ground ... which in memory have been dry and firm ... now surrounded (for the most part) by water'. Men tried to stem the tide, but seemed to be fighting a losing battle. So strong was the adversary that flood defences were often short-lived: a sluice at the Horseshoe, below Wisbech, never got the chance to prove its worth, as it 'stood not seven days, but was broken and blown up by the tyde'.

This, then, was the land that King Charles I decided to reclaim from the waters – not an easy task for, as Defoe later observed, 'All the waters of the middle part of England that do not run into the Thames or Trent come down into these Fens'. Undeterred by the size of the undertaking, the King ordered the draining of the Fens. The task, entrusted to a Dutch engineer called Cornelius Vermuyden, was not without problems and setbacks. Nevertheless, the job was finally proclaimed complete in 1652, and for a few years the Fens seemed once again a lush and prosperous place.

But it wasn't going to be that easy. Within thirty years the waters were back – and with a vengeance. Vermuyden's draining had created new problems, as the peat that underlay his new rivers, embankments and sluices began to shrink through loss of water. And during dry periods, the surface of the land dried into fine particles of topsoil that were picked up and blown away by the strong Fen winds. As the land shrank, the rivers were soon running higher than the fields around them. It was something of a vicious circle. Because water could no longer drain properly into the rivers, these weakly flowing watercourses soon became clogged with silt, making matters even worse.

By the end of the 1600s serious floods were commonplace. In 1673, the area between Spalding, Crowland and Wisbech was under three feet of water; and floods tore a 60-foot-wide hole in a bank of the Bedford River near Sutton Gault. The situation got even worse in the 1700s. Wisbech was under attack from regular flooding again. Houses disappeared under the inundations, and livestock was taken to higher ground. In 1713 Denver Sluice, an essential part of the drainage system, was wrecked by storm and not rebuilt until 1750. This, of course, caused even more flooding, and an enquiry of 1726 reported 'The Level is intirely drowned ... the Rivers ... lie higher than the lands: the Rain waters often drown the same Level.'

Man brought in reinforcements to aid his fight against the floods. Windmills arrived and were soon to be seen all over the Fens, pumping the water up into the rivers, so that it could flow once more to the sea. By 1748 there were 250 windmills in the mid-Fens alone. All the same, they didn't entirely solve the problem, and further inundations in 1770 resulted in flood water up to six feet (1.8 metres) high near Thorney.

The arrival of steam brought great improvements. In the early 1800s the windmills were replaced by steam engines, which were much more efficient at pumping water up off the Fens and on to the sea. These were in turn replaced by diesel and subsequently electric pumps. Finally the vision of past adventurers and drainers was realized. The Fens supported vast fields of healthy and profitable crops. Once the 'Drowned Lands', they had become the 'Breadbasket of Britain'.

Constant maintenace and improvement of flood defence mechanisms since then has largely kept the waters at bay. For all that, the cyclical nature of flooding on the Fens has not been tamed. Major floods bested even modern defences in 1936, 1937 and 1939. And in 1947 nature had a decisive victory. The floods of that year were caused by a freak combination of heavy rainfall, excessively high tides and a sudden change in temperature which melted the snow lying on the land in March. This unlikely sequence of events resulted in the most horrendous freshwater flooding for over 100 years. Nearly 25 square kilometres of the Fens were drowned; some villages and farms disappeared under as much as 6½ feet (two metres) of water; hundreds of families were made homeless, and thousands of sheep, cattle, pigs and poultry drowned.

What was it really like to be at the mercy of rising waters, knowing that there was no escape and that the best hope was mere survival? Those familiar with flood on the Fens often refer to the war against the waters. Reading the tales of those who lived through the events of 1947, war does not seem too strong a word. The following accounts by flood survivors and rescue workers, talking to a BBC Radio Cambridgeshire crew in 1997, chronicle the approach of a flood and the consequent destruction.

The siege lasted just over two weeks, and it took years to undo the damage. It all began in early March after the longest, wettest and hardest winter in living memory. Much of Britain had seen severe frost and heavy snow, and at times, the ground had been frozen 18 inches (half a metre) down and covered by snow drifts over six feet (two metres) high. This freakish winter weather, which lasted for about six weeks, set the scene for the terrifying events of the next fortnight.

10th March
- Sudden rapid thaw sets in.

11th March
- Heavy rain. Melting snow and ice combine with the downpour to create an effect equal to four-and-a-half inches of rain.
- Water begins to run off the ground (which is still frozen underneath the surface) at a tremendous rate, pouring into the rivers, which rise alarmingly.

14th March
- Flood patrols are by now on full alert, sandbagging and installing other emergency flood defences. Water leaks out of the tops of rivers in the Uplands. The flood is on its way.

> The road looked very much like a battleground, and the enemy was already at the gates. Lapping against the base of the sand-bag barrier with a sinister rustle, it could be heard against all the other sounds of the frantic activity going on. I remember thinking how the battle-like atmosphere was heightened by the noise of the mechanical forces engaged. As I watched, the barrier rose slightly faster than the rising floods. Watching with me were groups of evacuees from the threatened fen – women and children mostly, for their men-folk were at work on the defences. Their faces bore the typical anxious look of the dispossessed.
>
> *Local journalist*

15th March
- 500 homes, shops and offices in Bedford and the Ouse Valley are engulfed.
- Downstream in the Fens, locals frantically prepare for the onslaught heading towards them. River men and local volunteers work feverishly to bolster the banks. A thousand men toil at what they already fear may be a hopeless attempt to stem the flow.

> The most difficult part was to get the fellows to lay the bags properly ... the fellows were inexperienced and laid them anyhow.
>
> *Repair team foreman*

- The waters continue to rise and make their inexorable way towards

38

the Fens. In places the rivers and floodplains are already up to six feet (two metres) higher than normal.

They eventually cried the town with a town crier. 'Would all the employed on the Postland Farms report to the Wash end for sand-bag work?' We worked down there until very nearly eleven o'clock, and all of a sudden [we] were packing the bags on the top of the bank ... and it just started to slip away with us ... the bottom just simply spewed out, and I just yelled 'Jump ... for God sakes, she's going.'

Farm worker

- Emergency repair and defence is hampered by the height of the waters. Tugs and barges are sent with cargoes of clay to strengthen the banks. Many cannot pass under the bridges, which have very little clearance now. Some sink. In all, eighteen barges and three steam dredgers are lost.
- Evacuation of homes and farms continues. Many find it hard to believe a flood of such proportions is coming, although they can see it moving relentlessly towards them.

It was just like, you know, the sea at Hunstanton. You could see for miles only water, water, and it getting closer all the time.

Local woman

My elderly aunt said to me, 'I want to go into Downham Market to get some food in case the bank breaks – got a feeling something's going to happen.' We stood there for a while [waiting for the coach], and all of a sudden such a shudder of doors, shudder of windows, everything seemed to shake. When we looked over the fen my uncle said, 'I don't think you'll get to Downham Market. The dam has burst.' And the water was absolutely gushing up at the back of the property ... terrible mess. Frightening. Very frightening.

Local woman

I saw some women going down the road with some drawers out of my chest of drawers. I ... said, 'You're doing your usual good deeds then?' And then I tore after them like mad, because I saw some small bundles tied up with pale blue ribbon. They were letters my husband had sent to me when he was in the Army. Of

course they were going to go to the public house next door to
read them and I thought, 'You're not having that fun,' so I tore
after them and rescued the letters.

Local woman

16th March

- Hurricane force winds strike. By early evening, the winds are
blowing at 70 m.p.h., with gusts of 98 m.p.h. Men, working
against time to defend their homes and livelihood, are blown off
their feet. They are forced to stop work and watch as huge waves
approach. Trees, sandbags and telegraph poles fly through the air.
Communications are cut off in many areas.

The wind was blowing about a ninety-five-miles-an-hour gale,
and the river was level full of water. Some of it was seeping
through the bank. ... I was frightened out of my life. I was think-
ing, 'That's going to blow and they'll never see me any more'. ...
I'll never forget that as long as I live ... that terrifying.

Farm worker

When we put the [sand] bags down, you couldn't hold them.
You see, they kept lifting ... water was lifting over on to the fen
and taking large pieces of the bank right out. The report came
through that there was another breach forming ... which was
going to trap us. We got across to the other side and found
that the water was deeper. It was impossible really to lift your
feet off the base of the bank. So you were kind of pushing,
slushing your way through the water and holding one another
up. By this time I was drenched through. I was shivering
through exposure to the elements. I walked along – well, you
can't say walked, because against the force of the wind you
could sometimes lay actually right into the wind.

Member of repair gang

- Families struggle to save their homes and belongings from the
coming onslaught. They frantically move their most valued possessions upstairs or to higher ground. Many are forced to evacuate.

One stream of people went one way with the men. The stream
coming the other way was the women and children on the
lorries with their furniture, and, right on top of the furniture,

would be a dog or a coop of hens. It was the most pathetic thing I think I've ever seen.

Women's Voluntary Service worker

We were told the river ... was breaking its banks, and we would have to get out ... You could see it in the distance, and we still hadn't got any furniture out. About ten o'clock the water was still coming across the fen, and we could see half a haystack coming with it. Suddenly a cry went up, 'These people aren't out!' ... Soldiers came in the house, they took all the furniture out the front door, put it all along the ferry bank – just stacked it along – everything: chairs, tables, piano. Everything was dumped on the side of the road. They hadn't got a lorry. Then it [the flood] finally got to one field away, and that's when I started watching it. And it came across into the dyke beside the garden, then overflowed. And that was when it got frightening.

Young flood victim

- The banks of the Great Ouse at Over, just below St Ives, give way to the flood. Unable to withstand the force of the oncoming waters, they simply 'blow' (the word is apt). Torrents pour through the broken banks on to the fen. This proves to be the most serious breach of the floods.

  I looked in the direction of the breach, and I could see the water coming through something like Niagara Falls. The foam from it, as it was plunging into the fen, looked terrific ... terrifying.

  Farm labourer

  [The breach] was a terrifying sight. Black, sinister water was tearing through the flood bank and pouring into the fen. It was about 90 feet wide and getting bigger and bigger.

  River Engineer

17th March
- The gale continues, undoing much of the emergency repair and defence work. Water is overtopping more and more banks.

  I was aged five. ... My father ... took me to Earith and stood me on a river bank which I knew quite well. Instead of the chocolate

41

black fields with cottages, houses and farmyards and a few trees, on this day all you could see was grey water with a few tops of chimneys and trees sticking out. ... It was the most terrifying sight ... and I have never forgotten it. ... It was so vivid and so enormous that it stayed with me.'

Lord De Ramsey, former Chairman, Environment Agency

- The first detachment of troops arrives, with some lorries and DUKW amphibious vehicles (known as 'Ducks' to the locals).

  We were asked by a farmer to save his valuable bull, which had been in three feet of water for over 48 hours. It was about two-and-a-half miles over difficult country which was under about six or seven feet of water in places. Having secured the bull with a rope through a shackle at the back of the 'duck', we pulled away. ... As a result of the weight of the wheat we had in the 'duck', and the old bull pulling from behind, we found ourselves bogged ... about 40 yards from land. We were stuck there for about three-and-a-half hours ... The bull was getting very worried, very excited, but we managed to get a pole on him, and he wandered down the street very happily with his owner, who was very grateful to get him back.

  Army Captain

- More banks begin to weaken, and further breaches are threatened. Floodwater leaks continuously through vulnerable spots.

  It was dark and cold as we carefully picked our way along the narrow top of the bank, with the flooded river just below the crest on our right and the Black Fen fifteen feet below us on our left ... My imagination wrestled with the certain knowledge that anywhere along hundreds of miles of fen river banks the awful pressure of this water might prove too great, and that it only needed one failure for thousands of tons of black water to pour into the fen and ruin the rich farmlands and crops ... I felt stunned and helpless in the presence of a disaster which I knew would take place within the next few hours or maybe even minutes.

  A District Engineer

- Men who by now have been working non-stop for a week are tired almost to the point of collapse. The soldiers take some of the brunt of the emergency, raising morale. Work continues round the clock.

22nd March

- With violent gales still blowing, the next major breach occurs, this time further down the Great Ouse at Southery, between Littleport and Downham Market.

> Later, on the Saturday ... We heard that the White House [a large local residence] was in danger of being washed away ... and already a piece had gone. So we went down and had a look ... one window had gone and the water was coming through. It was just like Niagara ... I mean it was terrific. ... It's hard to describe. You really have to have the sound ... the power of that water coming through here, and this massive house wasn't going to stand it. ... About ten o'clock, 'cos it was dark and there was search lights on the south field where they had been digging the earth to fill the sandbags ... they played the searchlights on the remaining piece – the wall of the house – and we saw a chimney start to wobble. Then not long after that, the whole wall tipped. Before it hit the ground it split into halves and then crashed into the water. Gone. ... Then we got a display. They [had] cut the electric cables but hadn't cut the telephone cables. So, as this wall hit the water, the telephone cables came back [and] hit the overhead electric wires. It was a marvellous display. It was purple [and] white flashes the whole length of the wires – sparks – and then all the lights in Southery went out.

Fen woman

- Meanwhile, millions of litres of water are still pouring through the Over breach.

> I looked out of my son's window and thought, 'Whatever's up?' They were tearing about down there. People coming down the road and running up the hill. There were hundreds of people about, it seems. They could see the weakness. The water was blowing up through our garden ... just as if it was coming out of rat holes – you know, like a fountain. ... The [hole got] bigger until – bang! The lot went. ... Before I could get out of the door, it came straight through the front door and out of the back. It

43

was just a huge rush. I had some trees along the drain – they were huge. They went like pea sticks.

Fen smallholder

- Mobile canteens are set up, delivering 1,000 meals a day to the workers. In some cases food has to be taken by boat to crews working in harsh and isolated conditions.

24th March

- A small victory. The Over breach is stopped. The materials used are unusual, to say the least. Several amphibious vehicles left over from the war are found at nearby Bluntisham. They are 18-ton *Neptunes* waiting to be disposed of as war surplus. A use is found for them: they are driven into the 50-metre gap at Over and sunk. There, covered with tarpaulins and sandbags, they finally stop that torrent.

We slowly moved forward parallel to the floodbank and began to feel the current trying to sweep us through the breach. The *Neptune* was pushed sideways, but stayed on the ground. We edged forward until we were dead opposite the middle of the breach and still the tracks gripped. Just at that moment, the engine spluttered and stopped. The sudden absolute silence, except for the noise of the water, was a little awesome and I wondered whether the *Neptune* would capsize if it was washed through the breach. ... The water looked cold, uninviting and dangerous. But the *Neptune* remained as firm as a rock and I knew that my idea was possible.

Engineer testing the use of Neptunes *to seal the breach*

- Severe gales, along with rain and sleet, continue.
- It is feared that further breaches will occur.

Below me lay what looked like a choppy inland sea bordered by a green grass beach. Land on either side and ahead was ... barely distinguishable from the muddy flood waters below. Yellow islands were the tops of almost submerged corn stacks. Feather patches were the higher branches of tall trees sticking up from the surrounding waters. Lines of telegraph poles rising from the floods like outsize mooring posts marked the route of inundated roads. Half submerged farms, grey and lifeless, dotted the landscape below, emphasizing the sense of cold desolation which this vast sea of water so grimly evoked. The only movement in this grey scene came from the white flocks of wheeling gulls.

Aerial reconnaissance observer

4th April
- The Southery breach is finally staunched with a massive brushwood and willow mattress and tons of clay.
- The weather is still dreadful. Emergency repairs carry on regardless, and, slowly but surely, the tide of war turns in favour of the Fen folk.

This was really hard work, and at first the troops I had working under me hated it. The weather was windy and the work wet, and at the end of the day no fewer than 30 shovels were missing. The theory, of course, was 'no shovel, no work', and it was all too easy to lose a shovel in that river. ... They really had no idea what it was all about. So I ... explained how important it was; that the gap should be closed as soon as possible, and that until it was we couldn't pump out the fen. Once they got the idea they really did work well. For two weeks, working three eight-hour shifts a day, we continued pouring clay into the gap until, at last, the first bags appeared out of the water. It meant the river bank was whole again. It was really quite a moment.

Foreman of repair gang

9th April
- At last, the gales begin to blow out. As the winds decrease, the floodwaters start to subside. The massive clear up can now begin.

You won't believe this, but when we got back to our house there was mud all over the walls. Four inches thick, it was.

Householder

We went down there in the boat. It was a rough day, and the waves were high. We managed to get down there and collected his chickens. One little bantam we could not get was left. We couldn't get down there no more until the end of June. When we got there we found the bantam in the horse's manger. It had brought up a lovely little brood of chickens – about ten I suppose. Still alive and all right after three months.

Smallholder

- The people of the Fens start to put their lives back together. Some 30,000 acres (12,000 hectares) of flooded land must be reclaimed.
- Pumping equipment is sent from Holland. More than 200 pumps are used to remove the flood from the Fens.
- Much of the land is far too wet for immediate planting. Other areas dry out in hard lumps that resist all efforts at tilling.

Although the flood wreaked tremendous damage to property, crops and livestock, miraculously, no human lives were lost. The battle was won – this time.

The saga of floods on the Fens is one that will never end. The 1947 floods were followed by another massive disaster in 1953. After that things calmed down for a while, until the cycle started again: 1998 saw devastating floods that were repeated in 1999, 2000 and 2001. Who knows what the next few years will bring? Another dry spell, or more years of destruction and loss? One thing is certain. The floods will continue.

3. Invaders and Indigenes

Britain is a country made up of all sorts of different peoples, many of whom originally arrived as invaders. These invaders often saw the Fens and East Anglia as a convenient doorway to the rest of the country. For competent sailors, it is only a short journey from Europe across the North Sea into the Wash, and from there, the Fenland waterways offer an ideal route into East Anglia.

Although not strictly speaking invaders, the first incomers may have been the Bronze Age Beaker Folk. However, as an agricultural people they probably had little interest in the Fens, which even then were wet. Next came the Celts, who arrived from Europe about 700 BC. Although they left no records, these tribes, the first to use iron, settled significantly in the Fens and around their edges. Several hundred years later, it was their successors who put up a spirited resistance to the Roman occupation.

The Romans

Rome first turned its attention to Britain in 55 BC, when Julius Caesar briefly landed an invading force near Dover in Kent. The next year he moved further inland, taking forts near Canterbury and St Albans. It is doubtful, however, whether his troops reached the Fens. In any case, they soon retreated to deal with problems elsewhere; revolt in Gaul and civil war in Italy kept the Romans otherwise occupied for another hundred years.

The next Roman invasion, however, was successful. In AD 43, the general Aulus Plautus established a bridgehead in east Kent, from which his forces spread out over the rest of the country. It would be another four years before the Romans thought about an onslaught on the Fens, though. This would have been a carefully considered move, for around there lived some of the finest horsemen and chariot-riders in Britain: the large Celtic Iceni tribe. The Iceni were spread out through parts of Norfolk and Suffolk, and certainly the area of the Fens came under their influence. In the heart of the Fens lived the Girvii, also Celts and also fierce fighters, stubborn and aggressively possessive of their lands.

In AD 47, the newly appointed Roman governor, Publius Ostorius Scapula, set out to subdue these fearsome tribes. The campaign was long and hard, for the Celts fought doggedly, but, as happened elsewhere, the superior organization and strength of the Roman legions slowly began to prevail.

The Girvii probably never really accepted Roman rule. They may well have been bested militarily, but they were incredibly insular, surviving in parts of the marshy Fens where no one else could even make their way, let alone a living. The Romans had little interest in the bulk of their territory – wet, treacherous and completely unsuitable for cultivation – so, the Girvii (the Breedlings) would not have been greatly affected by the Roman occupation. The Iceni, however, occupied the higher lands, which included areas suitable for growing crops to feed the Roman legions. After years of fighting, the Romans established a client kingdom of the Iceni, under Prasutagus. However, in AD 60 Prasutagus died. He had directed that his lands and fortune be divided between his heirs and Rome: half to his wife, Boudicca, and their two daughters, and half to the Roman Emperor, Nero.

Prasutagus may have thought this a good political compromise, but the Romans did not. Whereas Celtic tradition allowed female inheritance, Roman society – chauvinist, if not misogynist – saw women as possessions. Roman women owned no assets and the idea that a woman could inherit goods, let alone a king's estate, was not acceptable. Besides, the Romans didn't want half the conquered land, they wanted it all. So they fell upon the Iceni and soon captured the kingdom, abusing and humiliating Boudicca and her daughters in the process. The Queen was bound and savagely whipped in front of her people, and some accounts say that she and her daughters were raped.

If the Romans thought that this would keep the Iceni in their place, they reckoned without Boudicca. A strong and proud woman of a fighting race, her reaction to this treatment was to assemble a hundred thousand Celts and strike against the conquerors. By all accounts, she was a fearsome leader. According to the Roman historian Dio Cassius: 'She was huge of frame, terrifying of aspect and had a harsh voice. A great mass of bright red hair fell to her knees; she wore a twisted torc and a tunic of many colours, over which was a thick mantle fastened by a brooch. Now she grasped a spear, to strike fear into all who watched her.'

Boudicca led her followers in fierce attacks against the Romans, telling her troops, 'Let us show them that they are hares and foxes trying to rule over dogs and wolves'. Her dogs and wolves burned three Roman strongholds – Camulodonum (Colchester), Verulamium (St Albans) and Londonium (London), and (according to Tacitus) killed some 70,000 Romans, including the 9th Legion. But such Celtic strength and ferocity was not sufficient to defeat Roman military power. Boudicca and her Iceni were defeated in battle, and the Queen died soon afterwards. Thus ended the last English resistance against Roman conquest.

The Fens were never again the site of any great Roman activity. No cities and few, if any, villas were built in the area – with perhaps one rather mysterious exception. In AD 130 the Emperor Hadrian built an enormous complex at Stonea, itself once an Iceni site. There was a fort and a palace as well as an administrative block, stable area, barracks and slave quarters. The centrepiece was a building measuring 80 feet by 30 feet and 60 feet high (24 × 9 × 18 metres). It had four storeys, four feet (1.2 metres) thick and painted to look like marble, and painted windows – a great luxury at the time. A sumptuous stone bath house had mosaic floors and an elaborate hypocaust. All in all, this was a Roman settlement in a very grand style, but its purpose is not clear. One interpretation is that the buildings commemorated the victory over the Iceni nearly a hundred years before. This theory is backed up by the fact that the Roman military camp at Stonea lay a short distance south of the complex; that camp may have been the site of a decisive battle against the Iceni. Another theory suggests that the buildings and tower were the residence of a Roman procurator who administered the Fenland area. In any case, whatever its origin, the complex was demolished around about AD 200.

The Fens chiefly served as a grain-growing area. The Romans made some limited efforts to drain the marshes and lowlands, but they valued the islands and fen edges for their rich soil, which produced wheat and barley, whereas the summer lands provided grazing for cattle, sheep and horses. Almost all the land was owned by the Roman Empire, with Fen farmers living as smallholders on short leases and paying tribute and tithes to the Emperor. Families lived in wattle-and-daub houses with clay floors. The fen-edge-dwellers and those on the islands enjoyed the Roman peace and profited from organized efforts to keep the land relatively dry.

The *pax Romana* came to an end in the fifth century. The Romans in Britain were never defeated, but were forced to withdraw to handle emergencies elsewhere in the Empire: Rome was under attack from barbarians from northern Europe and, once again, civil war threatened to tear the Empire apart. Troops were recalled, in 406 the last Roman legion left Britain, and the Dark Ages began. The civilizing influence of Rome quickly dissipated, and in the Fens, sluices, embankments, sea walls and other drainage devices were neglected. It doesn't take Nature long to undo Man's work, and the land quickly became drowned once again. An extended period of severe inundation followed.

The Anglo-Saxons

There were soon new conquerors on the Fens. Indeed, the Anglo-Saxons had begun invading as the Roman strength in England faded, and they were making forays into the Fens and elsewhere even before the last Imperial troops departed. Some were actually invited into England by Romano-British chiefs who enlisted their aid as mercenaries to fight off another invading force, the Picts from Caledonia. The mercenary troops were successful in this, but, instead of taking their pay and going home, they stayed and took over England by force.

The invading tribes consisted of Saxons, Jutes and Angles, who came from North Germany and Denmark. They soon took over much of England, with a significant presence in the Fens. Like others before them, they were mainly interested in the higher islands and fen edge, so the Breedlings and their descendants were, as ever, largely left to get on with their strange and hard lives. Inhabitants of the higher lands adapted to the new rulers, growing grain and keeping cattle and sheep. The conquering tribal kings ruled over the three social classes of noblemen, freemen and slaves in their separate territories, and by 650 there were six of these king-doms, one of them East Anglia. The years of relative peace and prosperity had seen the conversion of the kingdoms to Christianity and the growth of the monasteries and abbeys, which became wealthy and powerful.

The Vikings

The next episode is ruthless and bloody. In 787 the first of the Viking raiders arrived, attracted by the gold and treasures in the Fen abbeys. The name 'Viking' comes from a Norse word meaning pirate or sea raider, and that describes perfectly the hordes who crossed the North Sea, first from Norway and Sweden and later from Denmark, to plunder England. They were merciless in their quest for booty; the monks who wrote the *Anglo-Saxon Chronicle* referred to them as 'the heathen' or 'the force', and there is no doubt that their ways were brutish and uncompromising.

These new invaders were to make the fullest possible use of the Fen waterways. Having crossed the sea in their longboats, kitted out for war and pillage, it was easy enough to travel inland, up the Fen rivers. Longboats only drew two to three feet (under a metre) of water, so the Ouse and its tributaries would have provided ideal access. Rowing or sailing stealthily up the waterways, they were able to surprise villages, monasteries and abbeys, and to burn, pillage, loot and massacre before the locals could muster to defend them-selves. And when and if reinforcements arrived, the Vikings could get away with their bounty and travel along the rivers to their next victims.

In 800 more Vikings arrived, this time from Denmark. For the next 70 years they terrorized the Fens, taking over East Anglia, along with Northumbria and York, and overrunning Mercia. Their prime target remained the wealthy monasteries and abbeys. In 870 the Danes plundered Crowland Abbey, robbing and setting fire to the church and massacring everybody, save three monks. Not content with such mayhem, they threw the bones of Crowland's hallowed saints into the fire. From there they travelled to Medeshamstead (Peterborough) Abbey where they again set fire to the church and killed eighty people, including the Abbot.

Merciless raids on Huntingdon and Cambridge followed; then it

51

was back to the Fens to attack the prosperous and prestigious abbey at Ely. The people of Ely had heard rumours of the raids and had more time to prepare than earlier victims; they put up a courageous fight, but they too were overwhelmed. The abbey was set on fire, and the Danes added rape to their list of atrocities, making terrible use of the nuns at the abbey, as well as killing both monks and laymen who rallied to aid their Abbot.

The Vikings were a feared and fearsome force. Hugh Candidus, a monk at Peterborough Abbey in the twelfth century describes them, with hindsight, but certainly echoing the emotions of those who suffered the raids, as: 'servants of the Devil, and like mad dogs and robbers ... burning cities, villas, young men, women and children ... all things they consume with robbery, fire and swords, taking care that none should live to bring tidings of this massacre....'

It wasn't often that local folk were able to resist the marauders. However, the villagers of Hadstock reputedly managed to catch a Viking after he had plundered their church. Merciless in their retribution, they flayed him alive and nailed his skin to the church door, where it stayed until Victorian times. Unfortunately, this local legend turned out to have been a piece of local PR, as recent DNA testing has shown that the skin actually came from a cow. All the same, the tale demonstrates the fear and hatred the Fen folk felt for the raiders.

In 878, King Alfred finally halted the Danes' expansion and concluded the Treaty of Wedmore, dividing England along the line of the old Roman road of Watling Street into Mercia to the south and west and the Danelaw to the north and east. As the name implies, Danelaw was under the rule of the Danes. Most of the Fens lay within the Danelaw, so the next period of Fen history is very much one of Danish rule.

Perhaps the most famous Danish ruler (who was actually King of England from 1016 to 1035) was Cnut (Canute). King Cnut is remembered now as a good ruler and very keen to encourage and support the Church (though it was said of him that in earlier times he had been happy 'to wade through slaughter to a throne'). Certainly he must have affronted ghosts of his recent pagan forefathers, who had brought unbelievable horrors to the churches who now called Cnut friend and patron. To one of the first churches to suffer Danish outrages, the abbey at Crowland, he gave a valuable golden chalice that stood proudly on the high altar. Thus, in a relatively short time, 'the heathens' who terrorised Fenland abbeys and towns became beneficent rulers. Many settled on the Fens, mainly the islands and fen edges, becoming a part of fen life and tradition.

There is a final sidelight on the long and bloody period of Viking invasion. In the nineteenth century when the remains of what was almost certainly a Viking longboat were found in the fens near Manea, a local farmer, John Harris, told a friend how he came upon it:

> I was gettin' wild flowers outer D'Arcy Lode and two things riz [rose] up and frit [frightened] me mortal bad. I thought they must be sarpents, but they were the stem and starn of a big boat – you would call it a ship. ... Grandfeythur laughed ... and sez 'Don't be frit. It's the fen wot's a-shrinkin', and these things look as if they wos a-rising up. ... A lot o' us pecked her apieces and dried her; she did for kindlin' all next winter. I reckon the boat belonged to some furriners wot used to sail about these parts.

And that was the end of the last vestige of the Viking invasion – the great ship kept a Fen family warm one winter. A shame, because no ship of that time has been found intact in England – and yet perhaps a fitting coda.

The Normans

The next batch of invaders were to come to realize the strength of Fenland resistance. After William the Conqueror won the Battle of Hastings and became King of England in 1066 there were still those who did not accept Norman rule. Many of these dissidents fled to the comparative safety of the Fens, where they could hide and plot their retaliation. And with these refugees came a great deal of money, for many were landowners and noblemen dispossessed by the Normans.

By 1070 the Fens were almost the only part of England still defying the Conqueror, and hundreds of rebels had taken refuge at Ely. At the time the climate was in a particularly soggy phase and Ely proved an ideal hideout. Those who knew how to get across the surrounding marshes, or who had allies to guide them through, could reach it, but enemy scouts and soldiers, without such knowledge, would have a very tough time getting through the treacherous bogs.

But those on the Isle were not planning just to hide – they had insurrection in mind. Plots were afoot and feelings ran high. Also in Ely was a seasoned veteran of guerrilla warfare, jealous of his own lands and fiercely patriotic to boot: Hereward the Wake – the semi-legendary defender of England and leader of the last stand against the Normans.

Hereward is believed to have been born on the edge of the Fens, at Bourne in Lincolnshire; certainly he held considerable lands and assets there. He is reputed to have fought campaigns in Ireland, Cornwall and Flanders and to have been known for his courage, audacity and considerable military skills, preferring to work with small bands of soldiers, taking the enemy by surprise. He was an interesting and complex character who appears to have combined admirable motives with questionable methods. He is believed to have helped the Danes attack Peterborough Abbey (again) in 1070 so as to keep its treasure out of the hands of the Normans. Since Danes killed several monks, stole the treasure and set fire to their buildings, Hereward's patriotism may have been more dangerous to his allies than to his foes. Nevertheless, he was charismatic, tall with fair hair and fierce grey eyes, and these attributes, combined with his reported great strength and determination, easily gained him support.

This headstrong patriot and leader of men was in Ely in 1070 when William the Conqueror decided the time had come to clean out the last remnants of dissent against his rule. But it wasn't easy to reach the Isle, surrounded as it was by treacherous bogs which could turn into man-swallowing morasses without warning; truly, Ely was well defended by its surroundings. Nevertheless, William was not to be deterred, and he caused a kind of floating causeway of tree trunks and reeds to be mounted on piles across the bogs. The Normans began their assault by creeping carefully across this floating, bobbing pontoon. However, Hereward and his followers had a trick up their sleeves, and they set the reeds alight. A typical Fen wind whipped the flames into an inferno, and thousands of the invaders were roasted alive; others, seeking to escape the flames by diving into the marshes, drowned in their armour. (One of the more fanciful legends surrounding Hereward suggests that this Fen blow was the work of a witch who favoured Hereward's cause. More likely it was simply the predictably unpredictable Fen weather at work again.)

This victory was soon reversed, however, when Abbot Thurstan changed sides. No one really knows why he did so. Perhaps he was sick of the carnage and destruction. Perhaps he was simply cutting his losses, recognizing that the Normans would inevitably prevail on the Fens, as they had everywhere else. Whatever the reason, the Abbot of Ely, along with several monks, turned traitor and showed the Norman soldiers a secret pathway across the swamps and into Ely; Hereward and his followers were routed.

Hereward escaped by boat to Norfolk and then back to his lands in Lincolnshire. From there he carried out a sort of guerrilla warfare against William for a time, but in the end, perhaps accepting the inevitable, he too made peace with William. He is believed to have paid for his rebellion with a term in prison, but was returned to his Lincolnshire estate. Thereafter not much is heard of him. Some believe he was murdered by a vengeful Frenchman, others that he died a natural death and was buried with his wife, Torfrida, at Crowland Abbey.[1]

The Original Inhabitants

A true account of the past is the tale of the people who lived it. History is not only about invaders; it is also about the invaded:

---

[1] The story of Hereward the Wake has become a folk tale to almost the same degree as that of the much earlier King Arthur. The various legends about him culminated in Charles Kingsley's *Hereward the Wake*, which, although based on historical events, is a work of fiction.

The basic tale of Hereward is as given here, but a few accounts claim that he was the son of Leofric, Earl of Mercia, and his wife, Lady Godiva. In this version, Hereward was a tall, strange-looking youth with long hair and eyes of different colours. He was a tearaway, who, as a teenager, led a band of similar wild teenagers who terrorized the Fens. In despair, his father asked the King, Edward the Confessor, to banish this wayward son, so Hereward continued his wild ways on the continent. In Flanders he met his wife-to-be, Torfrida, a wealthy lady and a sorceress. The supposition, therefore, is that the witch said to have helped Hereward to fend off the Normans at Ely was his wife – but the witch is one of the more obviously mythical elements of the Hereward story. One thing that does seem to be known about Torfrida is that she eventually took the veil at Crowland Abbey. Also documented are that Hereward's father and brother were murdered by the Normans, and that he inherited estates in Lincolnshire and became Lord Bourne.

those who, like the Fen reeds, bent before the wind, then straight-ened up again and assimilated the incomers. And more important than legendary figures who fought great battles or carried out dramatic exploits are the ordinary folk who lived the ordinary life of their time, day by day, year by year, century by century. The first such people we know of are a mysterious race known by some as the 'Breedlings', about whose isolated and secretive way of life it is often only possible to surmise and suppose. One thing is certain, though: the Breedlings were the first to learn to live on the Fens, and their spirit permeates Fen history.

They were a race of small, dark men originating, possibly, with the first Celtic invasion, centuries before the Romans came to Britain. (Their origins may go back even further – to the Beaker Folk who arrived with their bronze tools more than 2,000 years before that. The majority of the Beaker Folk are thought to have kept to the higher, more prosperous lands, but perhaps there were some who preferred solitude and an independent way of life.) As early as the fifth century there are references to a dark and inde-pendent people called the Gyrwe living in the Fens, Celtic names are noted in local monastery and borough records, and there are references to 'Welshmen'. When the sixth-century monk Gildas wrote 'they alone persist in their faith, and in the lands of their fathers', he may have been referring to the descendants of Celts who had refused to be pushed westwards by later invaders and who clung on in their inhospitable and watery world of the Fens.

It is interesting to note that, along with the Iceni of Norfolk, among those who followed Boudicca in her attempt to defy the Romans was a tribe from the Fens called the Girvii – probably the ancestors of the Gyrwe. Perhaps some of those who joined Hereward the Wake in his heroic battle against William the Conqueror were their descendants, and the inheritors of a tradition of resistance to invaders and 'foreigners'.

The Breedlings conquered the Fens in their own way, making no attempt to change the nature of the land, but developing a way of life that turned the watery conditions to their advantage and living on the islands created by the constant flooding. There was a price to pay for this victory, though. Life was harsh, with disease and hardship a daily companion, and isolation inevitably led to in-breeding and distrust of strangers (surliness is too often mentioned in connection with these early Fenmen to be an exaggeration).

The Breedlings and their descendants were never centre-stage in the story of the Fens. They were not the Romans' representatives, nor the barons fighting for the Magna Carta; they were not the monks and bishops who ruled the land for so long; they were certainly not the aristocracy who sought to gain from the potential of the Fenland. They were not even those who tilled the land: they were an isolated, untrusting tribe who made the most of often horrific conditions in the 'Great East Swamp', and by doing so made it their own.

It was an alien land, with strange bird calls coming from the woods, overhanging foliage blocking out much of the sunlight, and, eeriest of all, ghostly glimmering lights caused by the marsh gases. Every day was a fight to survive in wet and sullen surroundings, but the Breedlings made good use of the bounties of the swamp: fish, eels and wildfowl. Another product of the marshes was less welcome, however; 'fen ague' (malaria) was a constant threat. Most Breedlings lived with the misery of malaria, as well as debilitating rheumatism and arthritis caused by their damp, dank living conditions, but, for all that, they were fiercely protective of their own land.

It was, of course, a fight they were bound to lose in the end. Inevitably, as more people came to the region, both invaders and settlers, the pure race of Breedlings slowly began to disappear. Whether they eventually accepted some 'foreign' intrusion and intermarried with the successive incomers over the centuries – Danes, Scots, Dutch, etc. – is not known. It seems likely, though, as there is no doubt that the spirit of the Breedlings carried on in the 'Fen Tigers', who opposed the draining of the Fens in later centuries. Today's Fenmen retain the tenacity of their predecessors, enduring the constant threat of flood and disaster. They are tireless in their vigilance, ensuring that flood defences are maintained and improved – and when, as is inevitable in their man-made land of plenty, disaster does strike, they clean up the damage and resume business as normal. The Breedlings knew how to make the most of their habitat. So do their successors.

4. Church and State

The Holy Land of the English

Both the Church and the Crown have played vital roles in the history of the Fens. Chronologically, the Church was the first to gain strength there, from the seventh century, when hermits began to find God in the dark, damp and disease-ridden Fens. What attracted religious folk to the unwelcoming swamps and bogs?

To answer this, it is necessary to understand the nature of Christianity at this time. Many believed that the end of the world, involving the second coming of Christ and the Day of Judgement was, if anything, overdue. They renounced worldly ways and considered anything that distracted them from their worship of God as a very real threat to their eternal souls. They believed earthly pleasures to be a sin, and saw suffering as their passport to immortality when Christ should return to collect his own. Of course, one of the best ways to escape the temptations of the flesh is to avoid them entirely by putting yourself somewhere completely beyond their reach – and the dank and dreary Fens were just the place for this. A man attempting to survive in that bleak land would have no time for mortal sin; it was just what many were looking for – a veritable hair shirt of an environment.

Not the first, but certainly the best-known of these hermits who made the Fens their home was a Mercian nobleman, Guthlac. Having decided to renounce the ways of the world and become a monk, he went to the monastery at Repton, but subsequently decided that the monks there lived too soft a life. So, in 699, he asked two brother monks to row him to Crowland, which at that time was known as Cruland.[1] He was prepared for what he was about to

[1] One of the suggested meanings of this name is 'a crude, rough and boggy land', so it isn't hard to see what Guthlac had in mind.

face, having been warned that Cruland was 'a certain island ... which many had attempted to inhabit, but could not for the strange and uncouth monsters and several terrors wherewith they are affrighted' (Dugdale). Some accounts say his servant, Beccelm, stayed with Guthlac for the fifteen years he survived on Crowland; apparently the saint-to-be wore crude animal skins and existed on a daily diet of a piece of barley bread and a cup of water from the muddy marsh.

The 'crude, rough and boggy land' was all he wished for and more. Quite apart from the difficulty of finding food and shelter from the all-pervading damp, he had demons to fight. 'Black troops of unclean spirits ... of form terrible, having great heads, long necks, lean faces, pale countenances, ill-favoured beards, rough ears, wrinkled foreheads, fierce eyes, stinking mouths, teeth like horses, spitting fire out of their throats, crooked jaws, broad lips, loud voices, burnt hair, great cheeks, high breasts, rugged thighs, bunched knees, bended legs, swollen ancles, preposterous feet, open mouths and hoarse cries' (Dugdale). Whether these demons were creatures of this world or another is impossible to say. Certainly there is a rational explanation for the terrors that visited Guthlac both day and night. He would undoubtedly have contracted malaria, and the resultant fevers would have been intense and probably accompanied by strange dreams and hallucinations.

There is a legend that Guthlac was visited by avenging demons, irate at his intrusion on to their island. They dragged him forcibly from his cell, took him to the very brink of Hades, and there threatened to cast him into everlasting torment for daring to invade their home. It is not outside the realms of possibility that these could have been the native Breedlings, always deeply resentful of 'foreigners' and fiercely protective of their isolated way of life; Guthlac's fevered brain could have turned them into demons – although they would have been pretty terrifying even without the delirious embellishment.

In time, Guthlac became a well-known and well-loved figure, caring for the Fenlanders, healing the sick, even taming wild animals. Eventually, he became a local legend: one of the stories that indicates his caring nature is that swallows returning to Crowland in the spring would go first to Guthlac, perching on his hand, so that he could tell them where to build their nests.

Guthlac's piety must really have been impressive, for his reputation spread, and he was soon receiving visitors, or perhaps pilgrims is a better term. One of these was Ethelbald, a minor dignitary from

59

Guthlac's native Mercia. Guthlac predicted that Ethelbald would become King of Mercia; the chances of that seemed slim, and Ethelbald did not believe the hermit, saying that if such an event should come to pass he would build a monastery at Crowland. Surprisingly, the prophecy came true in 716, two years after Guthlac's death. Nevertheless, Ethelbald kept his word and building of the monastery began the same year. Soon the monastery at Crowland was one of the most powerful and wealthy abbeys in England, and Guthlac was made a saint.

Shortly before Guthlac battled with his demons in Crowland, another saint in the making had begun the ecclesiastic tradition at Ely. Princess Etheldreda (or Audrey), daughter of King Anna of East Anglia, was another devout Christian who shunned the temptations of the flesh. To her, chastity was of the greatest importance, and as a girl she vowed that her soul and body would belong to Christ alone. Nevertheless, as the daughter of a King, she could not hope to escape political marriage, and she was married at an early age to Tondberht, a prince of the Gyrwe, thereby cementing a powerful alliance for her father. However, she managed to get her prince to agree to a chaste marriage. On his death in about 655 she retired to the Isle of Ely, which had been part of her dowry, to lead a chaste and devout life. However, this did not last long, for around 660 she was married again – this time to Egfrith, King of Northumbria, to cement another political alliance for her father. Egfrith, who was only fifteen at the time, agreed that she could remain a virgin. Twelve years later, though, he thought better of the deal and demanded his conjugal rights. Etheldreda escaped him and fled back to Ely, where in 673 she founded a double monastery, consisting of both nuns and monks, restoring an old church that ultimately evolved into Ely Cathedral.

Etheldreda succumbed to the plague c. 680, along with several of her nuns, many of whom were sisters or nieces. Contemporary reports say she died of a tumour on the neck, which some fancifully interpreted as divine punishment for her vanity in wearing necklaces when younger.[2] Seventeen years after her death her body was

---

[2] Possibly apocryphal is the belief that the word 'tawdry' derives from the often cheap and inferior necklaces of silk and lace sold at St Audrey's Fair in Ely (originally St Etheldreda's Fair and held around her feast day). The tatty laces or ribbons were believed to be holy, having touched her shrine, but were cheap and ill-made.

found to be uncorrupted and in perfect condition – miraculously, the tumour on her neck was healed, and the burial cloths in which she was wrapped were clean and fresh. Etheldreda became a saint, and Ely, like Crowland, went on to become a major abbey on the Fens – by 970 one of the richest in England, and second only to Glastonbury.

By 800, Christianity was firmly established as the religion of England and had a firm hold on the Fens. Mercian and East Anglian kings granted the monasteries large tracts of land and Fenland estates – a fairly trouble-free way to demonstrate their devotion to God and at the same time to establish control over the wilderness areas. The Church went from strength to strength, exacting tithes and rents and accepting offerings from king and commoner. A century after its foundation in 969, the Abbey of Ramsey was recorded in the Domesday Book as the largest single landholder in the country, owning sixteen manors outright, as well as portions of eight more.

The growth of the monasteries brought prosperity and civilization to the surrounding lands. Unfortunately, as we have seen, it also brought invaders. Viking raiders, hungry for new conquests and riches, heard that across the North Sea there were monasteries with jewels, silver, gold and money. They were certainly the richest places in the Fens and, better still, they were poorly defended, having little but the monks and a few local inhabitants to protect them. The Viking raids – which began in 787 and continued until the Danes conquered East Anglia and killed its king, St Edmund, in 869 – had a tremendous effect on the churches. In 870 the raiders attacked Crowland Abbey and then went on to sack the abbey at Peterborough, which was already famous throughout the Continent as a seat of great learning. Ely, too, fell after a great struggle, its monastery being almost completely destroyed and not restored until 970.

But the Church was not that easily beaten, and, as more peaceful conditions returned, the great houses began to regain their power and strength. This rebuilding suffered a setback when the King of Denmark, Sweyn Forkbeard, invaded in 1010. Fortunately, his son and successor Cnut was of a gentler nature – or perhaps, as King, he could afford to encourage the monasteries rather than sack them. Certainly he was well-disposed to the monasteries and visited Ely, Ramsey and Peterborough often; he even came to be known as one of the fathers of English church music, as he encouraged the monks to investigate new musical forms.

> Merrily sang they, the monks at Ely,
> When Canute the King he rowed thereby;
> Row to the shore, men, said the King
> And let us hear these monks to sing.

Edward the Confessor was educated as a child at Ely, and other royal children were to follow suit. In the first half of the eleventh century, the abbey at Ely was arguably the foremost in East Anglia, if not England (some would bestow the honour on Bury St Edmunds). The Domesday Book records that it owned 150 acres of land at Nutford in Norfolk and another 550 acres near Wicklow in Suffolk, in addition to local fen lands.

Domesday Books. The Norman census ordered by William the Conqueror in 1086 was in two parts. The second book, 'The Little Domesday' is believed to have been transcribed by monks at Ely

The latter half of the century was a great period of expansion for the monasteries, as religious orders came from the Continent after the Norman Conquest. In the Fens, the Benedictines were the strongest order, though the Cistercians and Augustinians were also present. Soon abbots were nearly as powerful as kings, and kings gave massive gifts to the abbeys, presumably to safeguard their immortal souls without going to all the effort and discomfort of serious piety. When Ramsey Abbey was founded it was given jewels and silver, plus the entire parish of Godmanchester; Peterborough was also known as Gildenburche (Golden Borough), because of its great wealth. The abbots were important noblemen, and thus became closely concerned with the fortunes of the monarchy.

A certain amount of religious rivalry was perhaps inevitable, as each pious community tried to out-build and out-saint the other. They fought over the ownership of land and control of the inhabitants. An old Fen rhyme aptly describes the characteristics of the major abbeys:

> Ramsey the rich of gold and fee.
> Thorney the flower of many fair tree.
> Crowland the courteous of meat and drink.
> Spalding the gluttons as all men do think.
> Peterborough the proud as all men say.
> Sawtry by the way, that old abbey
> Gave more almost in one day than all they.

Crown and conflict

Ely probably had more connections with royalty than any other abbey – and more dissension. One of the earliest of these conflicts took place in the twelfth century. Henry I's son and heir had predeceased him, so when the King died in 1135 the succession was in dispute. Despite Henry's wish that his eldest daughter Matilda should become queen, his nephew Stephen of Blois proclaimed himself king. The old king's Treasurer, Bishop Nigel of Ely, supported Matilda's claim to the throne and rallied supporters and strengthened Alrehede Castle at Ely. However, he was betrayed by an Ely monk and forced to escape into the Fens before joining Matilda in the west country. Stephen seized the assets of the bishopric and redistributed them amongst those loyal to his cause.

Needless to say, this caused a great deal of bad feeling amongst the dispossessed who began to gather again in Ely. Stephen called upon the Earl of Essex, Geoffrey de Mandeville, to quash the incipient rebellion, which he did with a vengeance, capturing Ely and using it as a base for raiding the surrounding countryside. De Mandeville may have begun his raids at the king's command, but soon he was simply lining his own pockets with the loot taken from the terrified locals. His methods were as ruthless as his allegiance was suspect. As the Anglo-Saxon Chronicle put it, he looted and raided 'sparing in his cruelty neither age nor condition. ... Christ and his angels wept.' Stephen was determined to put an end to the atrocities and mounted an attack against Geoffrey, putting the outlaw and his gang under siege by erecting a string of garrisoned strongholds in and around the Fens. It was at one of these (Burwell, Cambridgeshire) that the robber baron met a rather ignominious end: taking a rest during battle on a very hot summer's day, he took off his helmet to cool down and was hit by an arrow. He died at Mildenhall shortly thereafter. The King and the Bishop of Ely were eventually reconciled, and the confiscated lands were returned to the Church.

Less than a century later, though, the powers on the Fens were once again at odds with the Crown. This time it was the barons who caused the trouble, infuriated by King John's abuse of power. He had defied the Pope and confiscated Church property, but what probably angered the barons even more was that John imposed increasingly unrealistic taxes on them.

In 1214 many Fen landowners and barons, along with other nobles, made a pilgrimage to the Shrine of St Edmund in Bury St Edmunds, a little way outside the Fens. There the Archbishop of Canterbury, Stephen Langton, presented a Charter of Liberties, the document which was to become the Magna Carta. However, John got wind of the meeting, and the barons were forced to flee to Ely, where they prepared for a siege. This time it was not a monk who betrayed them but the fickle Fen weather: the rivers froze and royal troops were able to cross the ice to Ely break the siege. Despite this, the rebels eventually prevailed, and John was forced to sign the Magna Carta at Runnymede in 1215.

John ought to have had enough of the Fens by then, but in 1216 he visited King's Lynn with a large retinue and was travelling on to Wisbech (some say Peterborough) when, according to the contemporary chronicler Matthew Paris, 'he attempted to force a passage over the water which is called the Welle stream, and there suddenly and irrecoverably lost all his waggons, treasures, costly goods and regalia. A whirlpool in the middle of the water absorbed all into its depths, with men and horses, so that hardly one escaped to announce the misfortune to the king.' Another report states: 'Then, journeying towards the north, in the river which is called

Spears, known as glaives, which were used for catching eels

A basket used for catching eels

Barrel-making equipment. Barrels were used for a variety of purposes from food and beverage storage to transporting eels

A sixteenth-century cottage in Ely

The house in which Oliver Cromwell resided in Ely, now the Ely Tourist
Information Centre

The old Bishop's Palace next to Ely Cathedral is now a Sue Ryder Home

Bridge at Crowland under which three rivers once flowed

Statue on Crowland Bridge –
believed to be of either St Guthlac
or Christ

Ruins of Ramsey Abbey gatehouse

A selection of spades used to dig out new rivers and drains

Inscription that once stood over the great Lark Pumping Engine. The stone now lies rather unceremoniously propped against a wall at the Prickwillow Drainage Museum

The River Great Ouse near Ten Mile Bank – the river on the right is higher than the road on the left of the bank

Geese – once the Fenman's treasure. Almost every family had a small flock of
geese which provided valuable feathers, as well as food

The Stretham Old Engine pumped water off the fields and into the rivers in the
nineteenth and twentieth centuries

Outbuilding at Downham Market showing the uneven sinking of foundations so typical of buildings standing on the shrinking peat of the Fens

The Old Rectory at Prickwillow. When the house was built the front door was at ground level

Wellstream, by an unexpected accident he lost all his wagons, carts and sumpter horses with the treasures, precious vessels and all the other things which he loved so well; for the ground was opened up in the middle of the waves, and bottomless whirlpools swallowed them all up.' There is debate as to whether this incident occurred on land or water. It is likely to have taken place some way inland and been caused by a tidal bore; these sudden floods, which rush with great violence up river estuaries, are known locally as shuffs.[3] Sadly for John, that was his last encounter with the Fens, for he died a week later at Newark.[4]

[3] The coastline has receded considerably since those days and the royal treasure probably lies under some farmer's field in the fertile Fens. Given that the Fens have been steadily shrinking since the seventeenth century, it is odd that none of it has ever been found.

[4] There is another version of the tale of the loss of the King's jewels, which, though unlikely-sounding does purport to explain his death so soon afterwards.

In this version, John decided to stop for the night at Wisbech Castle where he took advantage of local hospitality and spent the night in the arms of a local maiden. But when he awoke in the morning he discovered that she, his servant and his treasure had all disappeared.

In the course of their getaway, though, the girl and the servant were held up by foot pads. Strangely, the gang decided that the pair should not have their throats cut but should join their band, and they would all share the spoils. They then concocted a little surprise for John, removing the treasure out of two of the bags and replacing it with the servant's livery. The bags were sent to John, who by then had reached Newark Castle in Lincolnshire. When he opened the bags and discovered the deception he was so infuriated that he had a stroke and died.

But the story doesn't end there. Apparently the thieves, complete with John's paramour and servant, lived in hiding for many years. Nine months after the event she gave birth to a boy (called, appropriately, Prince), who went on to become one of the most feared robbers on the Fens. However, the rest of the band perished when their hideaway was overwhelmed by a freak flood that drowned both them and their ill-gotten gains. (Until recent times there were said to have been sightings of a ghostly young woman between Welney and Littleport at Gold Hill, the presumed site of the flood, searching for her lost loot.)

In the seventeenth century the treasure was unearthed by Dutch workers digging one of Vermuyden's drains. But they were set upon and killed by the Fen Tigers who were so opposed to this work. These Fenmen presumably divided the loot up amongst themselves, and that is the end of the story. Needless to say, there is no evidence for any of this.

The thirteenth century was a time of civil unrest and change across England, and the Fens played no small part in this. By the 1260s the barons were at war again with the Crown. In 1266 supporters of Simon de Montfort calling themselves 'the Disinherited', determined to regain land and assets they had lost to John's successor, Henry III, turned Ely into a base for raiding into Cambridgeshire, Norfolk, Suffolk and parts of Essex. For a while the rebels succeeded, repelling blockades and raiding the uplands; in fact, so successful were they that the taxable value of Cambridgeshire plummeted from over £200 to nothing in 1267. Finally, however, they were defeated, thanks once again to the fickle Fens weather: this time it was an unusually dry summer that allowed royal supporters to cross the marshes and fight their way through to Ely and victory.

After that the Crown seemed to have an easier relationship with the Fen dignitaries. Ely, in particular, became a favourite royal visiting place; both Edward I and Edward II frequently stayed at the Bishop's palace. Perhaps the rulers had learned their lesson – from then on they took great care to choose Bishops of Ely from among their most loyal supporters.

The next upheaval, the Peasants' Revolt of 1381, was largely an insurrection by the common folk against their rulers. The collectors of the poll tax that had been imposed in 1377 were probably the most obvious enemy, but the higher clergy and lawyers were equally disliked. One key figure in the insurrection was Adam Clymme of Ely. Not a man to mince his words, he said of lawyers: 'No man of law or other officer in the execution of his duty should escape without beheading.' He is also reported to have stated: 'No man of whatsoever condition he were, free or bond, should obey his lord to do any services or customs, under pain of beheading otherwise than he should declare to them on behalf of the Great Fellowship.'[5]

East Anglia and the Fens were among the areas most affected by the Peasants' Revolt. In the Fens the action centred mainly around Ely, and there were also sporadic outbreaks of rioting in Littleport. These were quickly put down by the Bishop of Ely, one

---

[5] Although there is little hard evidence, many believe the Great Fellowship to have been the organization behind the Revolt. There were men who travelled the country stirring up unrest and these could have come under the Fellowship's control. Certainly Adam Clymme himself was 'always wandering armed with arms displayed, bearing a standard to assemble insurgents'.

of the fighting bishops of the time. A far cry from the hermit monks who had started the religious tradition on the Fens centuries earlier, these churchmen had a very different agenda. *Ex officio* owners of vast acreages of land, and with a considerable income from crops and cattle as well as rents and tithes, these bishops were far from spurning worldly ways and were keen to retain and increase their control, both economic and political. Presumably, they were also not averse to taking up arms to safe-guard their interests, even though, as men of God, they were forbidden to spill the blood of other men. They found a way around this by riding into battle in full armour and bearing maces instead of swords; clubbing their enemies to death, they main-tained, avoided the blood-letting involved in a sword cut. (It has to be said that clubbing can't always have been a bloodless death, but this sophistry must have been enough to assuage the fighting bishops' questionable consciences.)

The Peasants' Revolt doesn't seem to have accomplished much for the common folk and, in the end, was compeltely quashed. The last of the rebels were routed out and dealt with harshly in Ely, Norwich and Cambridge by Bishop Despenser of Norwich and the Abbot of Ramsey, presumably two more Christian soldiers who, if they didn't wield swords themselves, had plenty of troops with them who did.

Meanwhile, the power and wealth of the monasateries continued to grow. Goods travelling from King's Lynn to the abbeys included tallow, rice, wheels and axles, wine and timber. And that's just what came from English sources; there was a steady stream of goods from abroad as well – wax from Paris and the Baltic, and iron and nails from Spain, while from even further afield came exotic products such as cloves, mace, frankincense, figs, raisins, ginger, nuts and sugar. Then came the Dissolution of the Monasteries. First Henry VIII closed 40 of the smaller monasteries, a move which would not have affected the great houses of the Fens much, although no doubt it gave them cause for concern. Then in 1536 he closed 400 more, and two years later he got rid of all the larger monasteries; in ten years he had closed all 800 monasteries across England. This process had enormous effects on England as a whole, but Fenland was particularly affected, because the Church had long been its largest landowner and the maintainer of its drainage works and flood defences. Control of the lands fell to various small landowners who exercised no central management; each owner was concerned only with his individual parcel of land. It took the Fens a long time to recover from the subsequent neglect of the water system.

The Church's influence had now declined, but there was still a great deal of royal interest in the Fens. Indeed, at the beginning of the seventeenth century Charles I not only approved the Earl of Bedford's plans for draining the Fens on a hitherto unheard-of scale (as we shall see in Chapter 7), he also drew up plans for a magnificent royal estate at Manea, in the heart of the Fens. It was to be known as Charlemont, and Charles saw it as a perfect retreat from the pressures and political intrigues of London.

Alas, Charlemont was never to be, because the King was soon overtaken by one of the major events in English history – the Civil War. Interestingly, the other key figure in this struggle, Oliver Cromwell, was born on the edge of the Fens, in Huntingdon, and owned land in St Ives and Ely. He, too, had an important influence on the great drainage schemes that changed the face of Fenland. But one undoubted result of the Civil War was to change the balance of power across the whole country. Never again was either Church or Royalty to have such a powerful influence. In the Fens, though, the most influential factor was still the same – the waters simply wouldn't go away.

5. Life Before the Great Drainage

For most of recorded history, until the great drainage works of the seventeenth century, the Fens were unforgiving – waterlogged, dangerous, full of nasty surprises – and hardly the sort of place people would choose to inhabit, given an underpopulated Earth with plenty of easier options. But perhaps that is too simplistic a way of looking at it. Those born in the Fens would have had little opportunity to relocate. Only in relatively modern times have people been able to relocate themselves with relative ease. Before that, most people lived their entire lives within one or two miles of their birthplace. So, for those born on the Fens, it would have been a question of making the best of what must sometimes have appeared to be a very bad job.

But how did these people's ancestors get there? And what of those who migrated to the Fens? It seems that the first inhabitants probably arrived in Neolithic times, when the land was very different. At that time the Fens did not exist and, in common with most of northern Europe, the area was heavily wooded. Hunting would have been the chief form of survival, and the number of inhabitants would have been low. The Bronze Age saw the first major population of the Fens. It was at this time that the Beaker folk arrived but they were mainly agriculturalists and cattlemen, and would have had little interest in the area. Others, perhaps the Breedlings, harvested the abundant fish and fowl and settled throughout the Fens, and by the end of the Bronze Age a population was firmly established. During the Iron Age few new settlers arrived, for by this time the land was too cold and waterlogged, and the great meres were forming.

The spirit of the early Breedlings that runs throughout the story of the Fens first surfaces in the Celts: the Girvii, the Coritavi and the Iceni – fierce warrior tribes who survived through their fighting skills and refusal to be beaten. The Iceni, of course, are best known for leading the last fight against the Roman invaders under the banner of their ferocious Queen, Boudicca.

Like much of Britain, the Fen natives were already becoming a mixture of many nationalities and cultures. Inevitably the Romans, who occupied the country for almost four hundred years, left their mark on the land and the peoples. In terms of building villas and fortresses, not a great deal of activity took place in the Fens, but the Romans did build flood defences and undertake drainage work that benefited the area. Local Fenmen were drafted to work on these and on the Roman roads that crossed the Fens.

The Romans were followed by the Anglo-Saxons, who swiftly became the 'native race'. They had little interest in maintaining the drainage and flood-control work that the Romans had undertaken, and the Fens soon reverted to marshland, full of muddy meres, bogs and morasses. In some places all one could see for mile upon mile was water and reedbeds. The slightly higher areas of land became virtual islands and were the only places where most people could sustain a living. Soon the few islands poking up out of the sodden Fens became isolated communities, each cut off from the others by miles and miles of marshes and meres. Inevitably, their inhabitants became increasingly insular, with all the negative results that implies. Despite distrusting strangers, they fought amongst themselves. Intermarriage was a way of life, and the resultant inbreeding led to unhealthy characteristics. Breedlings indeed!

There is, however, a legendary figure from Anglo-Saxon times who proves that not all was darkness and distrust. Folk tales tell of Tom Hickathrift – truly a giant of man, over seven feet tall and phenomenally strong. He is said to have killed another giant, a robber, using the axle of his cart as a club and the wheel as a shield. Confiscating the robber's loot, he became a champion of the common people – a prototype Robin Hood – and he is credited with freeing the country from savage beasts and robbers.

The Normans came next, and they too had little interest in drainage, so the land remained much the same, and the Fenlanders' isolated way of life continued for centuries, earning them the reputation for being unfriendly and violently mistrustful of strangers. But what the Normans did bring with them was feudalism: a system under which all the land in England was owned by the king. Next in the hierarchy were the Church and barons, who were called tenants-in-chief; they were given land by the king in exchange for taxes and providing knights to fight the king's battles. And the tenants-in-chief often granted land to knights, in return for military services or guarding their baron for forty days per year. Below knights came the yeomen who, although free men, worked several days a week for the baron or the Church. Finally, the great bulk of the people, the serfs, provided the tenants-in-chief with crops in return for protection. These peasants were not free men, they were owned by their tenant-in-chief. They and their families could be bought and sold at will, and they could not even leave their village or get married without permission.

That looks like a fairly major change in the form of society (and indeed it was, in much of England), but one wonders whether it really had a great effect on the men of the Fens, whose land and life were so foreign to everyone else. As late as 1586 William Camden described them in his *Britannia* as 'a kind of people according to the nature of the place where they dwell, rude, uncivil and envious to all others whom they call Upland Men; who stalking on high upon stilts apply their minds to grazing, fishing and fowling. The whole Region itselfe, which in winter season and sometimes most part of the yeere is overflowed by the spreading waters of the river Ouse, Grant, Nene, Welland, Glene and Witham, having not loades and sewers large enough to voide away'. Certainly there was not much agriculture in the Fens then – life revolved around wildfowl, fish and eels.

In terms of historical records, the greatest Norman innovation was the Domesday Book, the great survey, instigated by William the Conqueror in 1086, to quantify his assets. This first census shows how little importance was placed on the marshlands: it seems to have almost entirely ignored the inundated areas and mentioned only the highland areas of the Fens. Data are recorded for such places as Witesie (Whittlesey), Mercha (March), Cetriz (Chatteris), Litelport (Littleport), Wisbece (Wisbech) and Dodinton (Doddington), but there is very little information about the water-logged Fens.

The Domesday Book aimed to record every manor and holding in William's kingdom (the word *dom* means assessment or judgement, so this was, in effect, the earliest census). The survey was painstakingly carried out and appeared in two parts. The first volume, describing most of the country, was most likely compiled at Winchester. The second part, known as the Little Domesday, is believed to have been documented by the monks at Ely. The monks were proud of the work, writing in the *Anglo-Saxon Chronicle* that 'There was not a single hide nor rod of land ... not an ox, a cow, a pig was left out', and it certainly gives us a good idea of the distribution of people on the Fens at the time. The silt fens in the north were the least populated, with two families and less than one plough team for every 1,000 acres (400 hectares) of land. The uplands, on the other hand, had twenty families and four to five plough teams for the same area, while the southern fens boasted six families and two teams per 1,000 acres.

Throughout the entire medieval period the Fens were home to two distinctly different lifestyles. On the islands and fen edges the economy was predominantly agricultural, as it was in most of the rest of England; cereals were grown as the main crop in hedged fields, and there were some vineyards, orchards and market gardens. The marshlands, however supported a pre-agricultural way of life, dependent on fishing, fowling and gathering reeds and rushes. Fish of many sorts, including perch, tench, bream, pike and even the royal sturgeon, were to be found in the rivers. Eeling was a massive industry, and indeed, eels were virtually a form of currency at times, 'sticks' of 24 being used to pay tithes and to purchase other commodities. (In the twelfth century, the villages of Doddington, Littleport and Stuntney contributed a massive 68,000 eels a year to the abbot-bishop.) The abundance of wildfowl and small mammals filled the tables of Fen-dwellers, and sedge, reed and turf (Fenmen have always referred to peat as turf), were valuable fuels, as well as building materials.

Perhaps it would be more accurate to say that there were three different ways of life on the Fens. For, although the uplands were mainly agricultural, and the lowlands survived on the products of the river and marsh, the summer lands combined both lifestyles. The summer lands are those areas which were wet for part of the year, during which time they were hunting grounds for fishermen and fowlers. In summer, though, they dried out and provided excellent grazing; often cattle were brought in by boat in the spring to graze all summer long. The farmers just had to be sure that they got the cattle out again before the first floods of autumn, for when the floods came early, taking all by surprise, entire flocks and herds would drown.

Although the ebb and flow of waters on the Fens has always been cyclical, for much of the time between the departure of the Romans and the massive drainage schemes of the seventeenth century, the pattern remained the same. There were dry periods, but these were the exception; the threat of flood was ever-present and the folk of the Fens never forgot how to survive in their drowned lands. A verse from 1662 describes the various occupations:

> The Toyling[1] fisher here is Tewing[2] of his net,
> The fowler is imployed[3] his lymed[4] twigs to set.
> One underneath his horse to get a shoote doth stalk,
> Another over dykes upon his stilts doth walk.
> There others with their spades the peats are squaring out
> And others from their Carres[5] are busily about
> To draw out sedge[6] and reed for thatch and stover[7] fit.

There was another common occupation not mentioned in the rhyme. The Fens were full of geese, with just about every family having a small flock. These birds were a profitable sideline, as they would forage for free on common land, and often flocks of a thousand and more could be seen pecking the fields and river banks for their food. These geese provided families with meat and eggs and were referred to as 'the Fenman's Treasure'. But, even more than for their eggs and meat, they were prized for their feathers, which made wonderful beds and quilts and could be sold profitably to town-dwellers. Sadly, the geese were poorly rewarded for being so productive. Their feathers were plucked five times a year, a process that was very painful for the birds and left them bleeding and raw; this practice continued well into the twentieth century.

Catching the abundant wildfowl spawned some pretty barbaric practices too. In the summer, the wild ducks moulted and were, for

[1] toiling
[2] preparing and dressing; working up; toiling or hustling
[3] employed
[4] covered in slimy or gluey material (as in bird-lime)
[5] copses in boggy ground
[6] a reed-like plant
[7] fodder

a short time, unable to fly. The Fenmen took advantage of this by forming a small army of boats and driving the ducks into funnel-shaped nets. This was a phenomenally successful method of catching the birds, as three to four thousand ducks could be caught in just one drive. Although a law was enacted in 1534 prohibiting the practice between May and August, the Fenmen paid no attention to it. They had families to feed and they did it however they could.

Life was hard and it was often short. Vast numbers of the population suffered from 'fen ague', which persisted until as late as 1850. It was described as 'an endemic incommunicable, paroxysmal fever' with a frighteningly high death rate, and was actually malaria, transmitted by the mosquito which thrives in stagnant water (little wonder it found a home in the Fens!). And rheumatism, although not fatal, made many a fen dweller's life a misery; it was by no means uncommon to see people crippled so badly that they could not walk upright. Nor was it just old folk who suffered: children were often maimed by the disease and lived the rest of their lives battling the pain.

Little wonder, then, that the Fen folk resorted to desperate means to combat these miseries. Is it a coincidence that the very conditions that promoted ague, rheumatism and arthritis also encouraged the growth of a flower that alleviated the symptoms?

Poppy Tea and Opium pill
Are the Fen cure for many an ill.

The poppy plant loves the wet fenland and grows there easily and in abundance. And the pretty little poppy is the source of a powerful drug – opium. The white poppy, also to be found all over the Fens, yields laudanum. People soon became aware of its pain-relieving properties, and the practice of chewing the poppies for this purpose was common for centuries. This illustrates the desperate need for some release from the pain of arthritis and ague. In fact, home-grown poppies could provide only a tiny proportion of the effect of that obtained from foreign flowers which were the true source of opium and its derivatives. The plant's highly addictive and sometimes fatal effects seem to have been largely ignored. Poppy-head tea was often given to children to help them through teething troubles, or simply to buy harassed parents a few quiet hours, whilst grannies used the potent brew to ease their pains and woes. This tea, or other poppy concoctions, were used for many ills,

not just ague and aching bones, and free and seemingly uncon-
cerned use of the narcotic continued until well into the twentieth
century, with the powerful drug widely available from pharmacists.

Fenmen had always excelled at coming up with ingenious solutions to the problems of life in their strange land. One can
understand that simply getting around could prove difficult when it
involved traversing treacherous bogs and crossing meres and rivers.
Many families had a flat-bottomed boat or a punt – which was
perfect for getting over the waters without snagging on the reeds or
running aground. Others utilized stilts and became very proficient
at travelling long distances swiftly and easily.

These talented stilt-walkers became known as Cambridgeshire
Camels – one of the more pleasant terms applied to the Fenmen.
Less flattering is 'Fen Slodger', though it certainly isn't difficult to
picture a Fenman making his way through cloying mud, each foot-
step making a 'slodgy' sort of sound. Yet another name has an
obvious derivation. While it is unlikely that the name 'Yellow-belly'
was intended to flatter, the modern meaning of 'coward' was not
intended; rather, the reference was to the belief that Fenmen had
webbed feet and lived like frogs. And it wasn't just the Fenmen's
ability to survive in a watery home that caused the comparison with
frogs: they were expert at jumping over ditches and drains and often
carried a sort of vaulting pole for the purpose.

However, neither stilts nor poles nor webbed feet would have
been much use once the water froze. The great Fen tradition of skating began as a means of getting over the ice in winter. Initially, the
skates were primitive, made of animal bones which were strapped
to boots; later, blacksmiths learned to make iron blades. For the
very young and the elderly, who did not have the necessary balanc-
ing skills, skates would be made that did not have a straight blade
but a circular one (imagine a pastry cutter); their wearers wouldn't
win any races, but they could traverse the frozen waters safely.

If skating across the frozen fens might sound like fun, other
methods of transport were not so pleasant. Often the rivers were
badly silted and only inches deep at points, which caused great
difficulty in moving goods via the waterways. A solution was to use
tow-horses that trudged along the river banks or waded ahead of
the boats, pulling cargoes from farm and mill to market. Often,
though, the owners of the land alongside the rivers resented the
horses trampling their land. The weight of several horses could soon

cause the bank edge to sink, leading to a potential risk of flooding. So sometimes it was men or even young boys who pulled the boats (sadly, in some cases, they came cheaper than horses). Often the human haulers would be waist deep in the rivers, pulling massive loads behind them. From time to time, the path or river would be blocked by a slough or dike or other obstruction, and when this happened the boat handlers 'were fain to take in the boy and the Horses into the Boat, and set them out again when they were past it, which was no small hindrance and loss of time, besides the death of so many Boyes and Horses with this unreasonable dealing'. It is not clear how this could prove fatal to boy or horse, but the wording strikes a chill note, for the writer seems more troubled by the 'hindrance and loss of time' than by the death of 'so many Boyes'.

Perhaps that is a key to early days on the Fens: life was cheap. There is no doubt that it was a hard world, made yet harder by the unpredictability of a climate that could bring years of plentiful summer grazing and bountiful crops, and then bring a devastating flood almost without warning. Although at times it was easier and at other times almost impossible, the Fenmen prevailed. The strain of obstinate survival running through Cambridgeshire Camels, Fen Slodgers and Yellow-Bellies harks back to the Breedlings who forged a way of life in conditions almost no one else cared to contemplate, let alone tackle. Yet, while the various names applied to Fenmen may be appropriate and certainly some are amusing, only one really fits the bill: Fen Tigers.

6. Early Attempts to Change the Land

A fen is defined as 'a low marshy land often, or partially, covered with water: a morass or bog'. Certainly that defines the East Anglian Fens at many stages in their history. However, for many centuries Man has tried to change the Fens to make them more hospitable and more productive. It must have been galling to see large areas of the land that seemed desirable places to live, capable of producing fine and abundant crops, often, mere weeks later, completely under water and the crops ruined. There was potential there, if only it could be realized – if Man could drain the Drowned Lands, tame the Fens and use the land to his advantage.

There were, of course, many who could already sustain an existence in the wet and unpredictable landscape. These were the true Fenmen – the Breedlings and their successors – who treasured the independent life the Fens afforded them and, seeing no need for it, resisted all change. But others saw the potential of the land and strove to improve conditions to their benefit. Over the years local landowners, the prosperous abbeys and even the Crown tried to make better use of the land. None of their attempts was wholly successful, for Nature resisted every step of the way, as did the Fen Tigers. Human nature, too, played a part in thwarting the schemes through neglect, poor planning and lack of organization.

From at least the thirteenth century those who attempted to improve conditions on the rivers were called 'undertakers' – literally those who 'undertook' river improvements. It is important to realize that there were two conflicting schools of thought. Some undertakers sought to improve drainage, enforce some form of flood control and enhance agriculture; others were concerned to improve river navigation and use of the rivers as commercial thoroughfares. Rarely did the two factions agree.

With early schemes, it is often unclear whether they were designed to facilitate drainage or the use of the rivers for transport and trade. The origin of much work that has been undertaken over the centuries remains unknown, and even today there are channels that are clearly artificial, yet their original purpose is not known.

The first undertakers of significance were the Romans. Most of their works were probably designed to improve navigation. The Romans had a massive network of cities, forts and garrisons throughout England, many of which were in and around the Fens. Hence, the rivers would have been essential for transporting goods, troops and provisions.

The most significant Roman undertaking was the Carr Dyke system, which ran for some 130km (75 miles) via Peterborough, to Lincoln. Believed to have been about sixty feet wide over most of its course, it was used to transport troops and goods. Even if designed as a navigational device, it certainly couldn't have done any harm as far as drainage was concerned, and, whether deliberately or not, it served as a catchwater drain where it skirted the western edge of the Fens. The Romans are also credited with building Soham Lode, Reach Lode, Swaffham Bulbeck Lode and Bottisham Lode. They also dug a series of channels in the northern part of the Fens which seems to have been excavated purely with drainage in mind. The Great Ouse north of Littleport was straightened, and this would have benefited the Wisbech area by diverting peaty silt in the direction of King's Lynn.

All indications are that during Roman times the land was dry and productive, and historical records show that the Fens were a fairly important area for growing corn and raising cattle. Some of this abundance can perhaps be put down to the cyclical climate of the Fens, but, as the Romans ruled Britain for almost four hundred years, it is more likely to be attributable to systematic attempts to drain the land and keep flooding under control. (These may have included Whittlesey Dyke and the Nene channel that runs through March.) Indeed the Roman writer Tacitus recorded that locals were employed on such work, and that they complained 'that the Romans wore out and consumed their bodies and hands in clearing the woods and embanking the Fens'. No doubt the Fenmen, who deeply resented 'foreigners' and jealously guarded their watery way of life, had a good deal to say about that.

A venture that would have used a great deal of local labour was one of the Romans' earliest projects, the Fen Causeway: a raised road, sixty feet wide, that island-hopped through the marshes from Peterborough to Whittlesey, then on to March and Denver. It enabled huge numbers of soldiers to be moved into or across the Fens, and, although we don't know when it was built, this road may well have been used by troops sent to subdue the Iceni – and we can still see parts of it today. Other Roman roads in the area include Akeman Street, running north from Cambridge and, just outside the Fens, Ermine Street, which was a major military highway connecting London to Lincoln and York.

Perhaps the most significant Roman contribution to making the Fens drier and more productive was to build a system of sea walls along the coast of the Wash to keep salt water off what they recognized as potentially productive agricultural land. These proved very effective, because otherwise fertile fields close to the sea could be ruined, if flooded with salt water: not only would that year's harvest be lost, but the land could be rendered useless for years to come. Once the walls protected these lands from the sea more food could be grown to feed the Roman troops.

However, after the Romans left in AD 406 the Fens quickly reverted to marsh and bog. By the end of the fifth century nearly all traces of the Roman works were gone, and the Fens reverted to a wilderness of floods and marshes that the insular Breedlings reclaimed as their own.

The first hermit monks, drawn to the seclusion and harshness of the Fens in the seventh century, were unlikely harbingers of the next attempts to civilize the Fens. They were the precursors of the abbeys and monasteries that by the eighth and ninth centuries had become affluent and powerful in the Fens, holding vast amounts of land. It was inevitable that they would seek to improve that land, effecting drainage schemes to increase productivity of crops and livestock. There was also considerable traffic in goods to and from the monasteries, so navigation canals were built throughout the Fens. Little evidence of these remains today, although it is believed that the Ely Cut, made sometime between the tenth and twelfth centuries, was one such monastic aid to navigation. There are also several thirteenth century references to waterways or drains called 'Monk's Lode'; the best known of these led to Sawtry Abbey.

King Cnut, a frequent visitor to the Fens during his reign (1016 to 1035), does not appear to have commissioned any drainage works, but he is reputed to have had King's Dyke built so that he could get from Peterborough to Ramsey Abbey without crossing the frequently storm-ridden Whittlesey Mere.[1]

During the hundred years between 1150 and 1250 many improvements were made to the Fen rivers and incredible changes occurred on the Fens. At the time of the Norman conquest in 1066 this had been one of the poorest areas in England, yet now it had become one of the richest, with populations increasing five- and even tenfold in some places. Individuals, groups of farmers and small groups of communities, as well as the wealthy Church, got together to implement drainage schemes, cutting ditches, raising banks and building sea walls. Other projects, such as building mills on the riverbank, improved conditions for those who used the rivers to transport their wares. However, the dams didn't suit farmers, because they often slowed the flow of the rivers, thus increasing siltation and flooding. The battle between navigation and drainage was old even then.

Then, as now, though, boom was followed by slump. By the mid-thirteenth century the economy began to collapse, and that, coupled with the arrival of the Black Death in England in 1348 (leading to the deaths of a third to half of the population) saw a decline in improvements. More to the point, landowners, including the Church, failed to liaise and organize, and there was little co-operation over maintaining existing river works, let alone starting any new ones.

That lack of co-operation frequently scuppered the best laid plans of undertakers. In the early thirteenth century, locals decided to open up what was probably an old Roman transport channel between Littleport and Brandon Creek to relieve flooding, which was particularly bad at this time, with lives, land and livestock being lost on a regular basis. Unfortunately, the results were not at all as envisaged. Previously the Great Ouse had flowed out to the sea at Wisbech through an outfall half a mile wide. The new channel diverted the river into the Little Ouse, so that both rivers now flowed into the sea at King's Lynn through an outfall only thirty

[1] Another story relates that, travelling from Soham to Ely one freezing winter, Cnut was wary of the strength of the ice he had to cross, and so hired a particularly stout local named Brithmer Budde to walk in front of his sledge. The ice held, and out of gratitude, or perhaps a sense of fair play, Cnut granted Brithmer and his descendants freedom.

yards wide – in no way sufficient to cope with the increased volume of water. Not surprisingly, this resulted in even more devastating floods, and banks were swept away. Another, delayed, effect was that the old course of the river leading to Wisbech silted up, resulting in more floods – this time from the various channels and rivers flowing into the Ouse. Wisbech, in particular, suffered from this gross miscalculation; in 1236 the situation was exacerbated by exceptionally high tides and winds, and eight days of massive floods caused more deaths. It was reported that in one village one hundred people were drowned in one day.

That is not the only example of mismanagement and lack of co-operation. Many river works were designed for trade or navigation purposes, and little or no regard was paid to the drainage implications. In one case at the end of the thirteenth century a dam erected at Outwell by Walter Langton, Bishop of Lichfield and Coventry, and designed to benefit his trade interests, led to flooding of 'lands, meadows, fens, turbaries [peat diggings] and a great proportion of arable', as well as 2,000 acres belonging to Crowland Abbey. Contemporary reports note that the devastation was such that 'the possessions of that monastery would not suffice to maintain the house, except the number of monks were lessened'.

The lack of central control did not pass unnoticed. King Henry III created a body of Commissioners of Sewers in 1258, appointing mainly chief local landowners to the task of co-ordinating and controlling undertakings on the rivers, drains and channels. The Commissioners had powers to oversee the maintenance and improvement of existing works, and they could ask landowners to undertake repairs and keep structures on their properties in good order. Additionally, the Commissioners were supposed to be able to order that river beds be dredged when they silted up. (Many mill-owners, etc., had built dams and bridges and weirs and fishgarths on the rivers, and, although these may have been of great benefit to their owners, they often seriously interfered with water flows. The idea was that the Commissioners could require the owners of riverside land to remove such obstructions.)

Unfortunately, from the very beginning the Commissioners had problems enforcing their powers. Obviously, funds were needed to maintain river works, but when the Commissioners set out to collect levies from landowners they were all too often ignored. It was easy to order an owner to repair or remove structures on the river, but much more difficult to ensure that he did so. The fact that the Commissioners were themselves local landowners didn't help matters; they were reluctant to get tough with their peers and offend their neighbours. Things improved somewhat in 1427, when the Commissioners were confirmed by an Act of Parliament and given the power to demand and collect taxes for repair and upkeep. Even so, and despite sometimes extremely zealous methods of collection, many local entrepreneurs got away without paying their due. In any case, the Commissioners were only ever concerned with maintaining existing works; they instituted no new works.

With little improvement or innovation, the inevitable flooded periods and drownings continued. In 1438 great plans were drawn up to dredge and widen the River Wissey and build two stone jetties within a hundred feet of the Ouse, but there is no evidence that this work was ever carried out. The next major scheme began in 1478 when John Morton, Bishop of Ely (and later Archbishop of Canterbury and Henry VII's Lord Chancellor) proposed a cut to carry the waters of the Nene from Peterborough to Wisbech more efficiently. This was a great undertaking that took twelve years to complete. Morton's Leam, a straight cut over twelve miles (19km) long and forty feet (12km) across, was completed in 1490.

Little more appears to have been instigated in the way of river works or undertakings until 1600, when the grandiose sounding 'Act for the recovering of many hundred thousand Acres of Marshes' was passed. But nothing much seems to have come of it beyond some marginal and not very effective reclamation in Ely, Elm and Soham. Then, in 1605, Sir John Popham, Lord Chief Justice, sought to drain the area around Upwell, and, like many undertakers before and since, assembled a group of associates, all of whom would presumably benefit from the work. Despite considerable problems, including opposition from the ever-resentful Fenmen, the group successfully dug a channel linking the River Nene to the Little Ouse; Popham's Eau, as it became known, still exists today.

The start of the seventeenth century saw the results of another long period of neglect and lack of co-operation. Once again broken banks and silted channels were causing almost constant flooding. The King, James I, turned his attention to the problem, declaring that the 'honour of his kingdom' made drainage essential. Sadly, his words were grander than his deeds. He tried to become an undertaker himself, planning to drain the Fens in return for 120,000 acres of reclaimed land, but the scheme failed due to lack of funds. The first of three government surveys was carried out in 1605 by two professional surveyors, John Hunt and Henry Totnall. Their findings were indicative of years of neglect. The depth of the Ouse at Ely was, in most places, not more than 14 to 18 inches (35–45cm), and between Ely and Littleport, the river had adopted a tortuous winding route that was disastrous for drainage. The Commission's proposals for a new cut to straighten the Ouse were initially well received but later shelved; apparently the plan was just too expensive.

But, of course, left to themselves, conditions did not improve. Indeed, flooding and consequent damage and death increased so much that in 1616 James had to instigate another investigation. A special Commission of Sewers under Sir Clement Edwards was appointed to report on the situation. It found things in a very sorry state and made sweeping recommendations calling for large sections of the Ouse to be 'cleansed, scowered, and perfected, to the ancient breadth and to the old bottom'. Further recommendations included removing all obstructions such as weirs, dams and gravel beds. All to no purpose. Contemporary reports indicate that the Commission was completely disregarded by 'self conceited, willful, and over-weening persons, out of their owne singularity and perverse dispoc'ons, not less dangerously threartening [sic] the iminent ruyne of those parts'. Vested interest is not a modern phenomenon.

In 1618 yet another survey was commissioned by the Privy Council to investigate the 'true' state of affairs. It reported that the area around Ely was 'generally fowle and overgrown with weeds, stopt with weare, and against Ely ... made shallow by gravell and fords'. It also looked at the outfall of the Ouse at King's Lynn and found it had now become dangerously wide and spread over a large area, reducing flows and clogging up the exit to the sea. Additionally, the size of the outfall meant that the sea could all too easily intrude upon the land, backing up the sluggish rivers to con-taminate arable and grazing land. The conclusion that it was vitally important to narrow and confine this channel was reinforced by another survey undertaken in the same year, in which Richard Atkyns stressed that the channel should be narrowed and confined as soon as possible. (It was to be two hundred years before anything along those lines was done.)

Nevertheless, real change was at hand. Despite the upheavals of the Civil War, a scheme that was to change the face of Fenland for ever was about to get under way.

7. The Great Adventure

Any history of the Fens can be divided into two distinct parts: before the Great Drainage and after. It's almost like looking at the story of two entirely different places (almost, because the spirit of the people – the Breedlings, the Fen Tigers – played a significant part both before and after). The Great Drainage was a hugely ambitious project conceived to convert the Great Eastern Swamp into reliable and productive agricultural land. By changing the natural landscape to one that met Man's needs and desires it irrevocably altered Fen life and even Fen geography. However, interfering with Nature is an arrogant and dangerous game, with consequences that are often unexpected and sometimes dire.

In 1630, a prominent local landowner set about implementing the perennial dream of creating a Fenland that was swampless – flood-free, fertile and profitable – and making the whole landscape (not just the islands and Fen edges) available for agriculture. Francis, the fourth Earl of Bedford, formed a band of investors, entrepreneurs and speculators who called themselves the Adventurers. The aim – to turn the Summer Lands, hitherto only available for farming during the few dry months, into year-round arable fields – was approved by King Charles I, and the massive project got under way, despite considerable opposition from the fishers, fowlers, eelers and reed-cutters who made their livings from the undrained Fenland.

The Adventurers needed someone with experience of drainage to take on what was clearly a massive task. They called on the services of a Dutch engineer who had been working in England for most of the preceding decade, Sir Cornelius Vermuyden. The key element of Vermuyden's plan was to straighten existing river courses and make new cuts, enabling the waters to run away to the sea more effectively. He had armies of navvies excavate a new channel 30km

(19 miles) long between Earith and Salters Lode, near Downham Market. This took the shortest route between two points on the Great Ouse, which had hitherto taken a lazy loop through the Fens further to the east via Ely. Vermuyden believed that a straight river – or drain, to use the Fenland term – would allow water to flow much more efficiently to the sea. The new route, which shortened the distance to the sea by 16km (10 miles), was an enormous undertaking, but Vermuyden had plenty of resources to call on, and the job was completed within a year. In 1631, the new channel was completed and named the Bedford River.

Other work involved later on in the scheme included making new cuts from Feltwell to the Great Ouse, from Whittlesey Mere to Guyhirn, from Crowland to Clow's Cross, and from New South Eau to Tydd. Additionally, Morton's Leam, which had become clogged with silt, was scoured to increase the flow, and sluices were built at Tydd, Well Creek, Earith and Wisbech. In 1637 the project was adjudged complete.

However, the best laid plans of earls and Dutchmen were soon to go astray. The snow and rain of the very next winter proved that there was still work to be done. The newly 'drained' land flooded, and conditions were, if anything, worse for the farmers than they had ever been.

At this point the King stepped in, intending to make himself the new 'undertaker' of the venture. Charles I had great plans for the Fens and even began designing a magnificent royal estate at Manea, to be built once the second stage of the drainage was completed. This time it was the King's plans that went awry, and he soon had much more to worry about than draining the Fens. Discontent and opposition to his rule was growing, and by 1642 he had a Civil War on his hands. Charles himself did not survive the Civil War, being executed by Cromwell and his supporters in 1649, but his plans for the Fens fared better. The drainage scheme was resurrected by the fifth Earl of Bedford, William, who had succeeded his father. An Act of Parliament of 1649 decreed that the new Earl should oversee work to drain the Fens, this time 'entirely', and the mistakes of the previous attempt were to be corrected. This time the aim was to control flooding all year round.

An engineer was needed, and once again Vermuyden was back on the job, extending the network of cuts and drains. A new river was cut, about 1km east of the previously created Bedford River and running parallel to it. This was named the New Bedford River, the earlier cut becoming known as the Old Bedford. (Apparently the similarity of the names proved rather confusing, so the New Bedford soon became more commonly, if unimaginatively, known as the Hundred Foot Drain – referring to its width). Other new drains included Downham Eau near Denver, Tong's Drain at Nordelph and the Forty Foot Drain north of Chatteris. And the first sluice at Denver, near Downham Market in Norfolk, was built; its primary purpose was to prevent salt water coming up the tidal river from King's Lynn from contaminating the Fen rivers.

The most important and innovative part of this new plan was the creation of the Ouse Washes. The area between the Old and New Bedford Rivers became a 4,700-acre (1,900-hectare) storage reservoir, designed to hold flood water until it was safe to release it into the rivers. Two enormous embankments were created to keep it in the reservoir: on the east, the South Level Barrier Bank, and on the west, the Middle Level Barrier Bank. The aim was to solve the problem of over-burdened watercourses that, during times of flood could not hold all the excess water and spilled it on to adjacent land, ruining crops and endangering lives. This water would now be held in the reservoir until the water level in the rivers dropped; then it would be allowed off the Washes and into the river system, to flow safely to the sea. Sometimes referred to as the Hundred Foot Washes, the Ouse Washes remain the key to controlling floods on the Fens, even today.

Work was completed in 1656 and, for the second time, the draining of the Fens was declared complete. For the first ten years, all appears to have gone as planned. There was still occasional flooding, but crops grew well, and there were bumper harvests. And then the floods returned. With a vengeance.

What Vermuyden and his colleagues had overlooked was the nature of the land. The area they had drained was almost 100% peat – and peat is 95% water. Draining that land caused it to begin to shrink, and hence to sink. Soon the peat lands, which had been five feet higher than the silt fens before drainage, were all lower than the surrounding land, in many cases below sea level. Worse still, although the peat lands shrank, the rivers did not, for their beds and banks were coated with deposits of sand that had settled out from the water flow. Thus was born the upside-down land that is the Fens today – with rivers running several feet higher than the land and fields around them.

Within thirty years of the final completion of the Great Drainage, the Fens were suffering disastrous flooding, and lives and livelihoods were being lost year after year. Things improved a bit when windmills were introduced to pump the water up off the fields into the river, and thence to the sea. But windmills were not powerful enough, and were far too dependent on the vagaries of the wind. Steam engines, which arrived in the early 1800s, did the job much better, and the situation improved still further with the introduction of diesel engines in 1913; automated electric pumps took over in 1948.

Pumping and the other flood-control measures detailed later in this chapter gradually turned the Fens into at least a semblance of what the Adventurers had envisaged. At great cost in time, machinery, maintenance and vigilance, the Drowned Lands did indeed finally become highly profitable farmland. They were never fully drained though, and never will be. There will always be floods; all Man can hope to do is predict them and minimize the damage. Comparing the Fens to a modern computer, it's as if the Adventurers, and all drainage undertakers before and since, have tried to change their default setting. It won't work, for that default setting is hardwired – an integral and unchangeable part of the mechanism. The Fens always want to revert to being Fens – swampland, marshland and bogs. Any small neglect by Man in continuing to build and maintain drainage and flood-prevention works will result in part of the land reverting to its natural state. Greater neglect would lead to the entire area becoming marshland again. That's the default setting.

Those are the bare facts of the great adventure of the seventeenth century drainage of the Fens. But these facts give rise to many questions. Were the Adventurers opportunists or altruists? What sort of man was Vermuyden? Was his scheme flawed, mismanaged or a complete mistake? Or was it a great success? The recorded facts vary between sources, and so, inevitably, do opinions.

The Adventurers

There is no doubt that in 1630 a group of landowners formed a syndicate to drain the Fens and that this venture had royal approval. There is, however, some uncertainty as to where the initiative originated. Some claim that King Charles had the bright idea and asked Francis, Earl of Bedford, to head the group to implement it. Another source believes that the King approached Vermuyden directly, promising him thousands of acres of drained land as his reward for doing the job. However, the Dutchman was so unpopular with locals that the King changed his mind and decided Bedford, who was a respected and well-liked gentleman, should be the figurehead. The most popular interpretation, and the most likely, is that the Earl of Bedford came up with a plan and approached the King for approval. Bedford was the largest landowner in the area, with approximately 20,000 acres around Thorney forming part of his estate. However it came about, the Lynn Law of 1630 granted the Adventurers corporate status, and the Great Scheme was under way.

There is doubt also about the composition of the corporation. Most say the group consisted of Bedford, plus twelve or thirteen other major fen landowners. There is a suspicion that Vermuyden himself was a member although it is unlikely that his contribution was financial. There is also the suggestion that some foreign money may have been involved. It is known that Dutch financiers had invested heavily in Vermuyden's previous two drainage schemes in England; however, these had been less than successful financially, so it is unlikely that foreign investment played any major part in Fen drainage.

Also unclear is how the proceeds were to be split. Some 95,000 acres (38,400 hectares) of potentially valuable land were up for grabs, if the scheme succeeded. The general consensus is that 12,000 acres (4,800 hectares) were to go to the King. And, sensibly, 43,000 acres (17,400 hectares) were to be set aside for maintenance, that is to say the revenues from this land would be used to pay for the upkeep of the works over the years. That left 40,000 acres (16,200 hectares) for the men who put up the money in the first place – the Adventurers.

But the first attempt at drainage, allegedly complete in 1637, proved a failure, and most, though not all, of the original Adventurers went bankrupt as a result (the Earl of Bedford appears to have escaped that fate). It is known that all the other members of the consortium relinquished all claims in 1638 – no doubt that was part of the bankruptcy process, for there can have been only liabilities connected to the venture at that point. The second attempt to drain the Fens, made in 1649, involved Francis's son, William, the fifth Earl of Bedford, and yet another group of Adventurers. But whether these included any of the original band is not known, although, after the financial pounding they took on the initial venture, it seems doubtful.

There is no doubt that the Adventurers were forward-thinking and rather brave. Although they could sit back and watch the navvies do the hard work, it cannot be denied that they were risking their reputations and their capital on what was undoubtedly a bold and rather uncertain venture. In addition to the logistical problems of drainage, there was a good deal of opposition to the scheme. Some of this was highly placed and influential, including industrialists who used the rivers to transport their goods and shipowners and navigators of all sorts. One particularly important opponent of the scheme was the administration of Cambridge University, which mounted massive campaigns against the venture: The University relied almost entirely on shipments carried on the rivers to supply its colleges and undergraduates, and, like so many opponents of the scheme, feared that the drainage would seriously hinder these arrangements.

The greatest opposition, though, and potentially the most dangerous, came from the ordinary Fenmen. Farmers might welcome the possibility of year-round agriculture, but the majority of those living on the Fens did not make their living that way. The Fenmen, sons of the Breedlings, feared the loss of their fishing, fowling and common rights; for them, a drained Fenland would be a Fenland in which eels would no longer be there for the trapping, there would be no more fish to catch, and the waterbirds would disappear. All the sources of their livelihood, which they had relied on for centuries, were threatened, and they responded accordingly.

Even before the scheme began there were protests, sometimes violent. A verse known as 'The Powtes Complaint', which first appeared in Armstrong's *History of Lynn* shows how they felt:

> Come, brethren of the water, let us all assemble,
> To treat upon this matter, which makes us quake and tremble:
> For we shall rue, if it be true, the Fens be undertaken;
> For where we feed off fen and reed, they'll feed both beef and
> bacon.'

They'll sow both beans and oats wherever man yet thought it,
Where men did row in boats, 'ere undertakers bought it;
But, Ceres, thou behold us now – let wild oats be their venture,
Oh! Let the hogs and miry bogs destroy where they do enter.

Behold the great design, which they do now determine,
Will make our bodies pine, a prey to crows and vermin;
For they do mean all fens to drain, and waters overmaster;
All will be dry, and we must die, 'cause Essex calves want pasture.

Away with boats and rudders; farewell both boats and skatches,
No need of one t'other, men now make better matches.
Stilt makers all and tanners shall complain of this disaster,
For they will make each muddy lake for Essex calves and pasture.

The feather'd fowl have wings, to fly to other nations,
But we have no such things to help our transportations;
We must give place – oh, a grievous case – to hornèd beast and
    cattle,
Except that we can all agree to drive them out by battle.

Wherefore let us all entreat our ancient water nurses,
To show their power so great as t'help to drain our purses;
And send us good old Captain Flood to lead us out to battle –
The twopenny Jack with scales on's back will drive out all the
    cattle.

The noble Captain yet was never known to fail us,
But did the conquest get of all that did assail us.
His furious rage none could assuage; but, to the world's great
    wonder,
He bears down banks, and breaks their cranks and whirligigs
    asunder.

God Œolus! we do thee pray that thou will not be wanting.
Thou never saidst us nay; now listen to our canting.
Do thou deride their hope and pride that purpose our
    confusion;
And send a blast, that they in haste may work no good
    conclusion.

Great Neptune, God of Seas, the work must needs provoke ye;
They mean ye to disease, and with fen-water choke thee;
But with thy mace do thou deface and quite confound this
    matter;
And send thy sands to make thy lands, when they shall want
    fresh water.

And eke we pray thee, Moon, that thou wilt be propitious,
To see that nought be done to prosper the malicious;
Tho' summer's heat has wrought a feat, whereby themselves
    they flatter,
Yet be so good to send a flood, lest Essex calves want water.

Once the drainage was under way the Fenmen did a great deal more than write poems and stage protests to make their displeasure known. They attacked work gangs, sent out night raids to tear down the previous day's work and set fire to construction sites. They did everything they could to impede progress, and did not stop at taking lives in the process. A confrontation at Wicken is described in Privy Council records: 'The people came out with pitchforks and poles, and gathered round a place where great heaps of stones were laid. Amongst them, John Moreclarke, a principal rioter, was charged to obey the Council's warrant. When the messengers approached him, he pushed at them with his pike. The people prepared to assist him, and the women got together a heap of stones to throw at the messengers, who were scoffed at and abused by the whole multitude.'

So the Adventurers had a great deal to contend with before the scheme got under way, and even more once it was in motion. To be sure, there were enormous profits to be made, but, like any scheme with great potential, it carried a high level of risk. As many have done before and since, the Adventurers suffered from the wrong end of the 'high risk, high gain' principle.

Why Vermuyden?

Cornelius Vermuyden was born in the 1590s in a small town in the Zeeland region of what is now the southern Netherlands, into a family that would have been the Dutch equivalent of wealthy Fen landowners. In 2001 Gerald Mains of Radio Cambridgeshire visited those living in Zeeland in a house that once belonged to Vermuyden's family and spoke to Rameen Marinus Bierens, who is related to the famous engineer. Bierens, a librarian, has done considerable research into his ancestor's life.

> He was born into a rather wealthy family – the Vermuyden family used to own several farms and pieces of land on the island of Tholen, where they probably did not work themselves; their tenants worked for them. They themselves lived in a rather big house in the town of Sint Maartensdijk, which literally means Martin's Dyke.

Cornelius is believed to have been the eldest son of the family, and therefore in line to inherit its lands and assets. So why did he leave Zeeland? Bierens has a theory:

> At that time, around the turn of the 1600s, the Netherlands were in very severe war to become independent ... what is popularly called the War with Spain. What really happened is that the Dutch wanted to become independent from the lords of the land; the Habsburgs, the Kings of Spain, were also lords of the Netherlands. Here we are quite close to the area where the war was being fought – in the south of the province of Zeeland and in the north of Flanders in Belgium. There it might have been more or less expected of him – coming from the background he did – that he would become an officer in the army. It is significant that during that war there was a ceasefire from 1609 until 1621, when both Spain and the Netherlands agreed not to make war ... and it is significant that just before the end of the ceasefire he went to England. So, very clearly, he did not want to take part in the war. He had been working as an engineer during the ceasefire – helping with reclaiming land in Zeeland and in the bit of Flanders which was being held by the Dutch. When the ceasefire came to an end he could not continue that work, because the area he had just reclaimed was becoming a battlefield again. So if he wanted to continue as an engineer ... he had to look for another job. And then came the invitation to work with the Court of St James in London.

This may explain why Cornelius left the Netherlands, never to return, and apparently turned his back on his family and his country. Although the people of the Fens see Vermuyden as a significant part of their history, virtually no one in his homeland knows of his exploits, and he is unknown in his home town. Bierens supports this: 'Only local historians would know his name'. When asked how it could be that Vermuyden is not famous locally, Bierens replies, 'Because he moved to another country.' He laughs, but continues seriously:

> Because he forsook his duty to be an officer in the army. It is not known that he ever came back – I haven't read anywhere that he ever came back for a family visit – so that is significant. He married in England to the daughter of a Flemish merchant – his first wife. And his second wife was English. He was a member of the Dutch Reformed Church at Austin Friars in London for many years ... Maybe he was not inclined to come back. Maybe he was not welcome.

So in 1621, aged 26, Cornelius left Zeeland and headed for England. At the time, his countryman, Joachim Liens, was already in talks with King James I about the possibility of extensive drainage works in England, and it is possible that Vermuyden came at Liens' invitation. Certainly he and Liens worked together on Vermuyden's first project in England, which was the drainage of the Dagenham Marshes on the Thames in 1626. It is not known whether Liens was involved in Vermuyden's next drainage job, the Royal Park at Windsor.

James I died in 1625, probably while the work on the Dagenham Marshes was still under way, and was succeeded by his son Charles I. Charles was obviously aware of Vermuyden's work for his father, and royal approval seems to have continued. After the project in the Royal Park was completed, Vermuyden was commissioned by the King in 1628 to undertake significant drainage works at Hatfield Chase in Yorkshire. Here there were 70,000 acres (28,300 hectares) of land not unlike the Fens, potentially valuable arable acreage that was regularly flooded and swampy. Vermuyden's engineering design involved draining the area and creating a washland – a reservoir to hold floodwaters. The principle was very similar to that which he later employed on the Fens.

This was a big project and, potentially, very lucrative. It is believed that Vermuyden had financial associates, including several Dutch capitalists and drainers, some English landowners and two British knights. They were known collectively as the 'Participants' – shades of the 'Adventurers' to come (indeed, it has been suggested that some Hatfield investors later became involved with the Fen drainage project, although there is no solid evidence for this). The Participants were to receive one third of the acreage of Hatfield Chase, a sizeable chunk of land.

From the very start the project was troubled by opposition from the locals, who, not unlike the Fenmen later, feared the loss of their livelihood and common rights and resented the 'foreign' intrusion. Vermuyden, who was described by a contemporary as a 'heavy-handed adventurer, with vision but lacking in finesse', ignored the protests. Most of the work was done by imported Dutch and Flemish workers, many of whom came to England on the promise that they could settle on the reclaimed land. This added insult to injury, and the locals rioted, destroying some of the work already done and killing several workers.

The summing-up of Cornelius's character by his modern-day relative, Bierens, seems to be confirmed in the Hatfield venture: 'He was a very vigorous kind of man who always wants to reach his goal. That part of his character can always be difficult for other people to deal with.' True, but it was no doubt also that part of his character that helped him to overcome the opposition and complete the draining of Hatfield Chase. This certainly seems to have been successful, as Charles knighted Vermuyden in 1629, primarily in recognition of his work at Hatfield.

Unfortunately, although the drainage seems to have been a technical success, the project itself turned into a rather messy business that resulted in Vermuyden's temporary fall from grace. Once the Hatfield work was complete, Cornelius was granted some 24,500 acres (9,900 hectares) of newly drained land. It was not a free grant, however, and he had to find £16,000 to pay for the privilege (it is believed that much of this sum came from the Participants). One of the conditions of the grant was the building of 'one or more chapels wherein the Dutch and Flemish settlers might worship in their own language' – obviously, although Cornelius would not or could not go home, he still hoped to maintain a part of his Dutch heritage. Houses and chapels and farms were duly built, for the settlers had every intention of living off the land they had reclaimed and making it their home.

Not surprisingly, the locals were once again irate; the common rights on those lands that they had enjoyed for centuries were being summarily stripped from them. More rioting and bad blood ensued. An inquisition into the whole affair was held, and the magistrates sided with the Dutch and the Flemish settlers. But Vermuyden, not satisfied with taking their lands from the locals, issued writs against many of them for damage to his properties. No doubt the damage was real, but the locals had little hope of paying, nor indeed any inclination to do so; several were sent to jail, and tempers rose even higher. More riots and destruction were inevitable. Vermuyden continued to demand compensation and the fighting, both legal and physical, carried on.

Authority stepped in again, this time in the person of Thomas, Lord Wentworth, Lord President of the North, who ordered that all litigation should stop. Vermuyden was not at all happy about this and continued to press charges and demand reparation. In the end, however, authority prevailed, and Vermuyden was forced to withdraw; in fact, he gave his land into the hands of trustees and eventually disposed of his interests altogether.

There followed another murky stage in the Vermuyden saga. It is almost certain that around this time Cornelius went to jail for a brief period. Whether this was for refusing to obey the edicts of the Lord President, or whether he experienced financial difficulties, is not known. It is strange, though, that he appears to have been jailed, knighted and asked to drain the Fens all within a period of one or two years. At all events, it was as the newly knighted Sir Cornelius Vermuyden that he was asked to engineer the draining of the Fens. He almost certainly embarked on the venture envisaging great personal gain, although in the end, it is very unlikely that he got much, if anything, out of the project.

After the work on the second Fens scheme was completed in 1652, Cornelius did another of his disappearing acts. Perhaps it isn't surprising that he lay low for several years after the drainage. After all, he was the engineer responsible for the works that soon saw the Fens shrinking and rivers spilling down into the adjoining lands. Moreover, he had never been well-liked, even by his peers, one of whom pulled no punches in vilifying the Dutchman for 'his misrepresentations, his system, his methods and his numerous failures'. What is surprising, however, is that Vermuyden seems to have vanished almost entirely. Almost nothing is known of him from

96

A replica of the gravestone marking the burial site of the five Littleport martyrs who were executed for their part in the Littleport Riots of 1816

Sheep stealing was a common crime in the nineteenth century and punished harshly, often with long prison sentences

FELONY.

Association for the Prosecution of all kinds of FELONY, within the Hundred of Ely, and South-part of the Hundred of Witch-ford.

Stolen or Strayed,

On Wednesday Night last,

OR EARLY ON THE FOLLOWING MORNING,

From the Ground belonging to Mr. BENJAMIN VIPAN, called or known by the Name of "SKEEL'S HUNDRED," near Welch's-Dam, in the Isle of Ely---

Nine Shearling Wethers, fresh in Condition, marked with the Letter (V) on the Rump, with Pitch, which is nearly worn out, some of them mark'd with a Slit in the near Ear, and others in the off Ear.

☞ *A Man was seen driving a small quantity of Sheep near the above Place, between 11 and 12 o'Clock at Night on which the same were lost.*

Whoever will give Information of the Person or Persons so offending, shall, upon Conviction of the Offender or Offenders, receive a Reward of TEN GUINEAS, if Stolen; and if Strayed, shall be rewarded for their trouble, and all reasonable expences paid, by the said B. Vipan.

H. PIGOTT, Agent.

ELY, September 22, 1825.

A scene in Ely Museum recreates the time when entire families lived in jail following the arrest of the father

Recreation and tourism play a growing role in the Fen economy of today

Dennis of Grunty Fen – a well-loved character, heard weekly on BBC Radio Cambridgeshire. Pete Sayers, as Dennis, pays a comical but affectionate tribute to the archetypical Fenman

Skates, typical of those which were used all over the Fens for day-to-day travel as well as competition

Display at Ely Museum. Members of the Women's Land Army were a common sight on the Fens during the Second World War, taking over much of the farm work previously done by men

Ramsey Parish Church of St Thomas à Becket

The river-front at Wisbech, showing the Dutch influence on architecture in earlier centuries

Along the Nene River at Wisbech

Organic flood defence mechanisms – cattle grazing on the river-banks help to
keep the rivers running freely and free of overgrowth

athedral

Sugar beet factory. The sugar beet crop was of major importance on the fens
during the twentieth century

The rich black peat of the Fens ready for planting

Horse-drawn apple cart used by an apple-seller near Wisbech

1652 until his death in London in 1677, although it is suspected that financial difficulties played a big part in his later life. It seems he was a bold, but ultimately not very successful, seventeenth century wheeler-dealer.

Arie De Vriet, a journalist from Vermuyden's native district of Tholen tried to find out about the engineer's later days, but was unable to come up with much, apart from confirming the date, if not the circumstances, of Cornelius's death. In another interview with Gerald Mains of BBC Radio Cambridgeshire, he said:

> The date of his death is known because he was registered in the burial, wedding and baptismal books of St Margaret's Church, where he was a member. The books are still held in the library of Westminster Abbey, because St Margaret's was changed to the Westminster Abbey diocese. So I went to the librarian from Westminster Abbey ... [who] was very kind to me and picked up a very big key and went down to the cellars of this library and came back with a very huge book. He showed me the real date, October 1677, when he [Vermuyden] was buried ... A cross was drawn near to his name. According to the librarian it meant that he was a man of importance.

Certainly Vermuyden was a man of importance to those who lived and are living on the Fens. But the question remains, was he saint or sinner, a crack engineer or a cowboy? Sketchley, writing in the late nineteenth century thought the latter: 'the main object Vermuyden had in view was to show how much better he could drain land than nature could, by doing all in his power to abstract the wealth of water and pour it into his own'. The fact that vast areas of the Fens today are covered by highly productive fields and farms does stem largely from the work done by Vermuyden in the seventeenth century, but is the relative success due to Vermuyden's own engineering skills or to all the work and expertise that has gone into solving the problems that his works created? The jury is still out.

Why did the First Scheme Fail?

After Vermuyden had excavated the (Old) Bedford River and made various other cuts and improvements, a Commission of Sewers was appointed to assess whether the task had been carried out success-fully. It met in St Ives, just on the fen edge, in 1637 to make its judgement, and it declared that the works were complete and satis-factory. It appears that the acres that had been promised to the Adventurers were awarded, although, interestingly, the 12,000 acres due to the Crown were held back. This would appear to be good news for the Adventurers, but they were also ordered to pay a Royal Tax on all those acres, amounting to a thumping £142,500 per year, so, given that the works had already cost them over £130,000, there was no great cause for celebration. Many people had been waiting to take advantage of the promised bounty of the newly drained land, and they quickly moved into the Fens to plant their crops and develop a whole new farming region. Unfortunately, their expecta-tions were not met. The onset of winter brought rains and snow, and there was dreadful flooding; the promised flood-free land was nowhere to be seen.

And yet Vermuyden had employed the principles he learned as an apprentice engineer in Holland – where, after all, they had had remarkable success in reclaiming vast areas of waterlogged land. So why did they not work in the East Anglian Fens? Well, the Dutch and English Fens, whilst looking remarkably similar, are, in fact, different in one vital characteristic. The Dutch reclaimed lands were mainly below sea level and with no natural drainage, whereas the Fens of East Anglia were (originally) almost entirely above mean tide level. In addition, they had good natural rivers to act as drains. Rameen Marinus Bierens, having studied his ancestor's methods, explains:

It was because in Zeeland he had been used to the fact that the level was absolutely flat. You were always one metre or so below actual sea level. Also the river estuaries are always close at hand. So, if he was draining a bit of land from shallow waters in front of the coast, he was always able to drain the water straight into the estu-ary – straight into the sea. But in England there was a different situation, in that he was draining land which was quite a bit upstream. It looks flat, just as flat as it is here, but it isn't; there is a very slight slope, which you don't notice. Therefore, when he was draining land upstream, it meant that downstream they would get too much water at once, and they had floods downstream where formerly they didn't have floods. So that was a problem he had to tackle. Here, the sea, or at least the estuary going to the sea, is always close, but in England the level was slightly higher.

There were many who were quick to blame Vermuyden, among them Andrew Bullard, contemporary landowner, who wrote, 'Sir Cornelius hath abused the King's Majesty and many of his loving subjects ... making hollow and counterfeit banks'. He additionally accused the Dutch engineer of using rotten timber for sluices, misusing the King's funds and taking lands illegally. Perhaps it was his determination to 'reach his goal', but there is no doubt that Vermuyden made many enemies in his adoptive home.

So, in 1638, only a year after the drainage was officially adjudged complete, the findings of the Commission of Sewers were declared invalid. The Adventurers had failed. And they paid the price. A subsequent Earl of Bedford wrote, 'All the participants were completely ruined, and the Earl's circumstances were much reduced.'

Was Cromwell Involved?

When one looks at the dates of the first and second attempts at drainage, it is obvious that the Civil War separates the two. Oliver Cromwell, the leading Parliamentary general and later Lord Protector, was born in Huntingdon on the edge of the fens, lived for many years in St Ives and then Ely and owned a great deal of land in the area. Add to that the facts that he was MP successively for Huntingdon and Cambridge, and that, amongst his other grandiose titles, he styled himself 'Lord of the Fens', and it might seem that he played a large part in draining the Fens.

Not really. His role was ambiguous and, it has to be said, some-what two-faced. Initially, he sided with the Fenmen who were so vehemently opposed to the scheme – indeed he used the cause to incite them further against the King. It would be generous to believe that this support was based on the fact that the gentry and the Crown, rather than the common man, might benefit from the project, but it is more likely that it was based on purely political reasoning: this was the common 'people's cause'.

After the Civil War, though, he did a complete about-face. Again, in fairness, it could be said that he was aware of the dreadful dangers of flooding and keen to do anything necessary to rectify the problem; or it could be that, once in a position of power, he could see the benefits of effective drainage and how he and his Protectorate could gain from it. Whatever the reason, he changed his mind entirely and gave full approval to the second scheme in 1649. As noted above, the Act granting this approval stipulated that the Fens be 'entirely drained' so that floods were controlled all year long.

The Second Scheme

Very soon after the first drainage it was obvious that further work was needed, and needed quickly. There is evidence to suggest that Vermuyden had the king's ear at this time and was active at court. He presumably sought to convince the king that the problems were not his fault and, more importantly, that he knew how to put things right. Charles was obviously convinced, and decided to become the 'Undertaker' of the Fens project himself, with a potential gain of 47,000 acres of new farmland. He was very enthusiastic and began to set things in motion, but then the Civil War drove all thoughts of drainage, or indeed anything other than survival, out of his mind.

After the war, during Cromwell's Commonwealth, the new scheme began. Francis, Earl of Bedford had died, and his title passed to his son William, who formed another group of Adventurers. Apparently, Vermuyden fought the new earl for leadership of the project, being unwilling to relinquish control (it is likely that King Charles had promised Vermuyden the right to call the shots on the next stage of drainage). However, with the King now executed, Vermuyden eventually had no choice but to agree that Bedford would take up the reins. He cannot have been very happy about this, nor about the fact that a ceiling of £100,000 was placed on the budget for the project.

The new Adventurers had a new contract. This time, the group were to share 43,000 acres (17,400 hectares) of fenland. There were 14 Adventurers, each holding either one or two shares, and there were 20 shares altogether. Of these 19 are accounted for, allocated to the earl and various landed gentry, but there is no record of who the twentieth portion belonged to – so perhaps Vermuyden was an official Adventurer again, holding the final share.

The works were again dogged by sabotage (at one point Cromwell had to send in a troop of cavalry to sort things out). As before, much of the work was carried out by foreign labour, in this case Dutch and Scottish prisoners of war. It is not difficult to imagine what the Fenmen, with their habitual hatred of foreigners, thought of that. Indeed, it is not necessary to imagine their reaction at all, as their protests are well documented. Irate locals staged raids on works that were under way and, in many cases, went armed to create as much havoc and destruction as possible. Newly built banks were knocked down; building works were vandalized and burnt. The Fenmen appear to have had little or no concern for the lives of the foreigners working on the project, for injuries and, sad to say, deaths were not uncommon.

Despite the difficulties, in 1656 the work was adjudged complete for a second time, and for a time, it seemed that things were better. For the first ten years or so, crops were successful, and soon there were good harvests of flax, hemp, oats, wheat, cole-seed, woad, onions, peas, corn and grass. But that was all to change dramatically.

What Went Wrong?

Within thirty years the Fens were once again consistently flooded. Rivers overflowed, embankments burst, crops were ruined and lives lost. Who or what was to blame? Some pointed the finger at the drainers, some at the Corporation for failing to keep the drains scoured. Others said that 'selfish' farmers put their neighbours at risk by draining their own lands too well.

Many blamed Vermuyden. A fellow Dutchman and engineer named Westerdyke believed Vermuyden's principles were misguided. Westerdyke insisted that rivers should follow their natural path of drainage, and that the answer to flooding was to remove the silt and debris from existing channels, rather than cut new ones. Another detractor, Sketchley, wrote in 1878, 'Vermuyden began badly, progressed ignorantly, and finished disastrously. These are strong words, but they are the honest outcome of long and practical acquaintance with the subject.'

Water lay on fields and farms, refusing to flow into the new river system. Worse, water spilled out of those drains, drowning crops and homes. Bewildered Fenmen thought that their rivers were rising – growing up from the bottom. What was actually happening was that the land was shrinking, an unforeseen consequence of the drainage of the peat.

Moreover, as the peat lost its moisture and shrank, the top layer dried out into a fine powder that was easily blown away. The Fens had always been subject to sudden and violent windstorms, but now these were more frightening and perilous than ever, for a severe blow could ruin a man. A farmer might stand surveying his newly-planted fields, perhaps counting the profits to come in a couple of months – but then, if a strong Fen wind got up, that same farmer would be left watching all his seeds, his income and his family's living for the coming year blow away. The windstorms were terrible to behold – great swirling clouds of dirt that darkened the sky, making it appear as if midnight had arrived at midday – and the dust that was blown around was incredibly fine. People would seal their windows and doors in whatever way they could to prevent the dust from getting into their homes; but, even so, by the time the wind died down, furniture would be blanketed in the stuff, and any food left uncovered would be ruined.

So, the problems caused by the drainage works had several facets. First the newly drained peat shrank, and the surface dried out, leaving fine particles of topsoil that were picked up and blown away by the strong winds. As the peat continued to shrink, the rivers began to run higher than the fields around them. The land could no longer be drained into the channels and instead lay on the fields, devastating crops. What water there was in the rivers ran slowly, leaving behind great deposits of silt that the current was not strong enough to wash away. By 1725 the bed of the Ouse, previously 14 feet deep, was in many places 'as high as the Soil of the Fens'.

Navigation interests, which had resisted drainage attempts from the beginning, were now able to indulge in self-righteous I-told-you-sos. In the early eighteenth century Thomas Badeslade described the drainage scheme as an 'ill formed, and still worse executed Project' responsible for the 'deplorable State of the Fens'. But the drainers had no time for the navigators either, claiming that the river men would happily 'sit undisturbed, though the roaring winds and the rushing floods threaten the whole Level with destruction', and they may have had a point. There is evidence that river-users were far more concerned with moving their cargoes than with the problems of the men who lived off the land. A good example of this attitude is an incident in 1763, when a large convoy of lighters carrying freight was being towed along the Hundred Foot River by a team of horses. The drivers of the horses, seeking to make better progress, began whipping the animals, which consequently panicked and tried to get away. As a result, the lighters swung against the bank of the river, causing a breach 60 yards (55 m) long and 33 feet (10 m) deep and releasing a flood that washed many a farmer's winter crops away and made many families homeless.

As far as navigators were concerned, easily the most hated feature of the new drainage system was Denver Sluice. It had been built by Vermuyden to accommodate the flows of no less than six rivers – The Old and New Bedford, the Great and Little Ouse, the Lark and the Wissey – and in many ways it was the cornerstone of his design. But there was no doubt that the sluice had its flaws. And these did not affect navigation only – drainage suffered too. When there were heavy rains, the water downriver got so high that the sluice could not be opened. This resulted in serious flooding in the South Level.

The complaints from river-users were frequent and forceful, ranging from petitions for the sluice's removal to violent attempts to demolish it. And the sluice was a terrific hindrance to their trade. The problems occurred year-round: in winter, the pressure of water against the sluice gates meant it was often impossible to open them to let the water out; in summer, drought frequently meant that the gates were kept closed to keep fresh water *in* the Washes. Boats could be held up there for days or even weeks, and the rivermen could do nothing but sit impatiently and wait as cargoes spoiled and their profits dwindled by the hour. Nor was it only the inconvenience that the navigators railed against – Denver Sluice was a dangerous place for boatmen. Sometimes, when the doors were finally opened, the torrent of water that came rushing out could capsize the vessels awaiting passage; boats sank and cargoes were lost.

In the end, Nature accommodated the navigators by wrecking Denver Sluice for them. In 1713 the spring tides came up river from the Wash while floodwaters rushed from the uplands down the Hundred Foot Drain. The two forces collided at Denver Sluice, which simply collapsed under the pressure. The subsequent devastation was dramatic. Soon the entire South Level flooded 'to such a depth that the sun cannot exhale the waters or dry them up. But that was not all. Within a few days, the silt deposits in the Ouse above Denver had increased by four feet, while downstream between Denver and King's Lynn, the river was no longer scoured by water flow and became disastrously clogged with silt and debris. Sea water got into the rivers and on to fertile fields, rendering them useless for crops for years. In fact, the incursion of sea water was so bad, that two years after the destruction of the sluice, a sturgeon 7 feet 6 inches (2.3 m) long was caught in Thetford Mill Pool.

And yet the anti-Denver contingent held out for years against the rebuilding: 35 years, in fact. However, the flooding just got worse and worse, and finally, after a particularly disastrous deluge in the 1740s, Denver Sluice was rebuilt. This time a navigation lock was put in, and the new sluice was of a better design, with wider waterways and lower foundations. In 1834 it was rebuilt again, this time to a design by Sir John Rennie which addressed and solved many of the previous problems.

So, for farmers, drainers and navigators alike, the eighteenth century was not a good century – sinking land, unnavigable rivers and, most of all, floods, floods and more floods. Daniel Defoe, in his 1724 *Tour Through the Whole Island of Great Britain*, noted, 'All the waters of the middle part of England which do not run into the Thames or Trent come down into these Fens ... We saw the Fen country ... almost all covered with water like a sea'. By 1800 things had still not improved, causing the writer Arthur Young to warn, 'two or three more floods will do the business, and 300,000 acres of the richest land in Great Britain will revert to their ancient occupiers, the frogs, coots and wild ducks'.

Technology to the Rescue

There was a great deal of drainage activity in the early 1800s. Bigger and better banks were built next to rivers, and the course of the Ouse was further straightened south of Littleport. A major project was the Eau Brink Cut made in 1821–2 between King's Lynn and Wiggenhall St Germans. (This was particularly needed, because previously, during seasonal flooding, men had had to balance on floating platforms to reap corn, horses had boards nailed to their hooves to stop them sinking into the fields and fruit was plucked off trees by men standing in boats.) More sluices were added to the system, including the rebuilt Denver Sluice, and new structures at Salter's Lode, the Hermitage, Earith and Welmore Lake.

But none of these improvements tackled the key problem of the sinking fens – that water does not run uphill. With the rivers now several feet above the land, this was a dilemma that had to be solved. To get the water off the fields and into the rivers, horse-drawn pumps had been tried, with very limited success. Then Englishmen had looked again to Holland for a solution to their problem, and found – windmills. Windmills, or 'wind-engines' as they were known, began to appear on the Fens in the seventeenth century, but did not become commonplace until the eighteenth century. The pumps were of a simple design: four or five sails to catch the wind and drive a waterwheel with a scoop, which lifted the water up and emptied it at the higher level. More ditches had to be built to take the water off the fields and transport it closer to the rivers, now hanging above the land. Then the windmills would pump the water up into the rivers. This was certainly an improvement. However wind-operated engines only work when the wind blows. Farmers were still the hostages of the elements.

It took new technology to solve the problem: steam. So long as the boiler fire is fed, a steam engine keeps on pumping no matter what the weather is doing, so, finally, Man began to have some control over the waters. The first steam engines were installed in about 1817 at Sutton St Edmund and Upware. By 1850 there were 60 operating in the Cambridgeshire Fens alone.

The Fenmen were in love with steam. On the new and impressive steam engine downstream on the River Lark they placed a great stone plaque with the following reverent, almost religious, inscription:

In fitness for the Urgent Hour,
Unlimited, untiring Power,
Precision, Promptitude, Command,
The Infant's Will, the Giant's Hand,
Steam, Mighty Steam ascends the Throne,
And reigns Lord Paramount alone.

These fens have oft times been by Water drowned.
Science a remedy in Water found.
The power of Steam she said shall be employ'd
And the Destroyer by Itself destroyed.

After that things only got better. The first steam engines had scoop wheels, similar to those on the wind pumps, but from 1851 these were superseded by newer ones with centrifugal pumps. The arrival of diesel engines in 1913 and, finally, of automatic electric motors in 1948 improved the situation further.

Of course, pumps didn't solve the problem. The Fens were still shrinking – indeed they still are. The extent of this shrinkage, over time, is graphically demonstrated by the Holme Fen Post which was erected near Whittlesey in 1851 by W. Wells, the man largely responsible for draining Whittlesey Mere, the last great Fenland mere, in 1848. He had the post sunk vertically into the peat so that the top was flush with the ground level at the time. By 1870 the top of the post stood 8 feet (2.4 m) above the ground; the height of the post had risen to 11 feet (3.4 m) by 1938. In 1960 a new post with a concrete base replaced the old one, but great care was taken to ensure that the replacement post stood at exactly the same level as the old; it is now more than 13 feet (4 m) above ground level. (The measuring post's site at Holme Fen is in fact the lowest place in England, lying more than 7 feet (2 m) below sea level.)

But it's not just the Holme Fen Post that dramatically illustrates the peat shrinkage. Many homes in the Fenland look like the work of drunken crazy builders; they lean this way or that, according to how the peat has moved underneath them. Some houses have doorways that are several feet up in the air; obviously, the current owners have built platforms so that they don't step out of their front door into thin air, but the evidence is still plain to see. A good example of this is the Prickwillow Rectory near Ely, whose front door is several feet above the ground. A house on the river bank at Littleport looks almost as if it were made of salt that has melted in the damp, to form a bent and squashed dwelling, the windows on one side leaning far to the left, those on the other to the right, and the doorway going in another direction entirely. It must be a very strange place in which to live, but it is inhabited still. A row of houses in Benwick play another strange trick. They were built with their fronts on an old gravel rodden (path or drove way) and their backs on the now shrinking peat. Consequently they lean backwards drunkenly and look as if they might topple at any moment.

8. Life After the Great Adventure

It wasn't just the topography that was changed by Vermuyden's drainage and subsequent refinements and 'fixes'. The Fenland way of life changed too. Previously agriculture had been mixed, although mainly pastoral, but now it gradually evolved into one based on arable farming. This proved a very desirable change for those who owned land in the Fens, as the newly drained and fertile land increased tremendously in value. As an example, 80 acres (32 hectares) of land near Ramsey, sold for £904 not long before drainage, were worth £3,200 by the late 1800s: almost a fourfold increase.

But the change was slow, and for several years after the Great Adventure people's lives continued much as they had for centuries. Traditional Fen industries such as fishing and fowling still supported many Fen dwellers, along with cutting turf and sedge. The

Fen Slodgers. For centuries the men of the Fens made a
living fishing and fowling

rivers, swollen as they were in the years following drainage, were full of fish: perch, tench, bream and pike – and eels, always eels. And sheep and cattle were still fattened on the summer lands. But it was, as ever, a hard existence, and many struggled. The diarist, Samuel Pepys, himself a native of the fen edge, visited relatives on the Fens in the latter half of the seventeenth century:

> Through the fenns, along dikes, where sometimes we were ready to have our horses sink to the belly, we got by night ... to Parson's Drove, a heathen place, where I found my uncle and aunt Perkins and their daughters, poor wretches – in a sad poor thatched cottage like a poor barn or stable, peeling of hemp, and in a poor condition of habit.

He ate with them at a local 'miserable inne', then

> to bed, in a sad cold stony chamber ... and so to sleep but was bit sadly ... by the gnatts. Up and got our people together, and after eating a dish of cold creame, which was my supper last night too, we took leave of our beggarly company, though they seem good people too; and over more sad fenns, all the way observing the sad life which the people of the place – which if they be born there they do call the Breedlings of the place – do live, sometimes rowing from one spot to another, and then wadeing.

Another contemporary report survives in the diaries of the eccentric aristocrat Celia Fiennes, who undertook a riding tour through England in 1695. In the Fens she was forced to make the journey between Ely and Sutton on the raised banks of the rivers, because all around her was flooded, and her horse almost tipped her into the river when it paused on a steep bank and bent to drink. One suspects she did not consider the trip worth the effort, for when she reached Ely she found it 'the dirtiest place I ever saw, not a bit of pitching in the streets except round the Palace and the churches. The Bishop does not care to stay long in this place not being for his health.' She described the Fen folk as 'a slothful people and for little but the taking care of their grounds and cattle' (though, given the miserable conditions in which they lived and worked, that must have been job enough, hardly meriting such criticism).

Away from the islands life was pretty grim. Many houses were ankle deep in water all winter long, and people survived mainly on fish and wildfowl, supplemented with butter and cheese if they grazed cattle on the summer lands. They used reed to thatch their houses. Due to the lack of trees, they burned peat and cattle dung for heating and cooking purposes. As we have seen, though, the Fen folk have always been a hardy lot who seemed, almost perversely, to thrive in seemingly impossible conditions.

An indirect result of the drainage schemes was a new element of the population. Many of the Scottish and Dutch workers who had been dragooned into digging the new drains stayed on in the Fens. Some already had their families with them, and others sent for their families to join them. To these immigrants were added, in 1652, Protestants from France and the Spanish Netherlands who were fleeing religious persecution in their own lands. Huguenots settled around Thorney, adding their own traditions and ethos to the mix that was becoming the typical Fenman.

Although the Fens were badly inundated for much of the eighteenth century, some benefits from Vermuyden's efforts were becoming apparent. Certainly the abundance of fish in the rivers meant a source of income for the Fenmen, who exported them far and wide. The closest major market was London, whither great quantities were sent overland from the Fens around Ely, Whittlesey Mere and Ramsey Mere. Defoe in 1724 describes how they were transported and kept fresh for the London markets:

This they do by carrying great buts fill'd with water in waggons ... the buts have a little square flap, instead of a bung, about ten, twelve or fourteen inches square, which, being open'd, gives air to the fish, and every night, when they come to the inn they draw off the water, and let more fresh and sweet water run into them again ... they chiefly carry Tench and Pike, Perch and Eels, but especially Tench and Pike, of which here are some of the largest in England.

As well as the fishermen, the boatman also saw better times. Initially, drainage measures caused them nightmares, but as the problems began to be dealt with, river navigation increased quickly. By the end of the eighteenth century there were approximately 67 'gangs' working the rivers (these were the crews that manned the cargo vessels). As an example, between May 1876 and February 1877, 7,070 vessels passed through Denver Sluice towed by 3,694

109

horses. As the barge trade grew, fleet owners became rich and influential, providing a lot of locals with work. Dr Ennion in his account of Adventurers' Fen noted: 'There was always something going on: a string of barges moving massively along the Lode, men loading turf, boys fishing.' Of course, the river men's prosperity was eventually wiped out by the railways, which took over their trade at the end of the 1800s. The fall was quick – the Wisbech cargo trade fell by half in just seven years after the opening of the St Ives railway line in 1847.

By 1750 East Anglia had become the most important source of grain and other crops for the London market, and by 1800 arable land had become more important than pasture in the Fens. Market gardens flourished in the highlands, where gooseberries, strawberries, raspberries, asparagus, cauliflower and blackcurrants grew well. Ely produced great quantities of greens and strawberries; Wisbech, although still in danger from unexpected flooding, shipped in an average year 13,000 hundredweight of oats, 1,000 tuns (approximately 220,000 gallons) of oil and 8,000 firkins (448,000 pounds) of butter to London. So, as always, it was a mixed picture, dependent on location within the Fens.

In 1774 Horace Walpole, third Earl of Orford, amused himself with a tour through the Fens by boat. Here he describes a typical Fen farmer at Upwell:

An active old man of seventy-five years of age supplied us with excellent milk for breakfast, and breakfasted with us himself on a bottle of Ringwood beer, which he commended much, and drank to the last drop. He occupied a farm of one hundred acres; kept seven milch cows. Farmer Rate was a brisk man of his age: had been twice married; had four children by his last wife, who was then living, and had four children by her first husband; she seemed of the same age with her husband, and to enjoy a good state of health, though sometimes attacked by an ague, the reigning disorder in these parts.

Indeed, the ague (malaria), sometimes called 'Fen Harr', was still very widespread in the Fens, and would remain so until well into the twentieth century, along with the arthritis and rheumatism described earlier. Fen folk relied heavily on opium and laudanum to ease their pain, and druggists in Wisbech sold huge amounts of

The demand was for cheap bread, and the rallying cry was 'Bread or Blood'.

In 1816, the situation for the poor on the Fens was dire. Grain prices had continued to rise, and so bread, which was all many subsisted on, was being priced out of the reach of countless workers and their families. In Littleport, on the banks of the River Great Ouse, 60 farm labourers met at the *Globe* inn to try to find a solution. To be fair, their thoughts were already turning to violence, for they were awaiting the arrival of men from nearby Southery and Denver, who had recently taken part in riots. But when these others failed to turn up, the men of Littleport decided to take matters into their own hands. Thus began a short but violent tale of social unrest, the legend of which lives on in the fens to this day.

Leaving the *Globe*, the aggrieved men, some of whom had no doubt unwisely spent what little money they had on ale, visited two of the most unpopular local landowners: one of them the vicar, John Vadell, the other Henry Martin, a wealthy and particularly despotic gentleman farmer. No doubt the threatening band of angry labourers was an unnerving sight that took the landowners by surprise, for it appears that they offered concessions, including cheap flour and wage rises. The men of Littleport took the landowners at their word. Some went home, and others returned to the inn. There they presumably began to doubt the sincerity of their betters, who had given in with suspicious ease, and to realize that all they had received was promises – and they had seen the empty nature of those before. Inevitably more drinking and complaining ensued, and later that evening the men decided to take action. Leaving the inn with mayhem in mind, they proceeded to ransack prosperous farmhouses and rob their owners.

The next day, still full of righteous fury, the Littleport men marched to Ely; they wanted the promises of the previous evening confirmed. At the head of the band were soldiers recently returned from the Napoleonic Wars, many of them out of work and hungry. It certainly wasn't a peaceful deputation, for they took pitchforks and shotguns, and a large-bore gun normally used for shooting wildfowl from punts was mounted on a cart to form a kind of cannon. They had more demands now, too: in addition to fair wages and affordable flour, they wanted cheap beer and a pardon for the violence of the previous night.

Confronted by this armed and angry band, the magistrates of Ely agreed to all demands. They issued an official statement:

> The magistrates agree, and do order, that the over-seers shall pay to each family Two shillings per Head per Week, when Flour is Half-a-crown a tonne; such allowance to be raised in proportion when the price of flour is higher, and that the price of labour shall be Two Shillings a day, whether married or single and that the labourer shall be paid his full wages by the Farmer who hires him.

Along with this, they gave the insurrectionists free beer. This was a questionable course of action when dealing with men who were already well oiled. But perhaps the calculation was that the free beer might well lead the men into further violence, placing them and their cause in a bad light. That is precisely what happened. Whilst some did return home peaceably, others fuelled by the dangerous combination of beer and righteous fervour, sacked shops and houses in Ely.

It is doubtful whether the magistrates' action had any purpose other than to get the rioters out of the way long enough for authority to mount a counter-attack. This they did the very next day, sending soldiers and cavalry after the men of Littleport. The labourers ended up barricaded in a pub, where they fought back as best they could against the superior force. Three soldiers were injured, but two labourers were killed and almost 100 arrested. Many more fled across the Fens, but were rounded up over the next couple of weeks, this time by Bow Street Runners as well as cavalry. They didn't stand a chance.

They didn't stand a chance when it came to the trial, either, for they were tried before the 'Hanging Judge of Wisbech', Edward Christian.[1] Twenty-four of them were sentenced to death – among

---

[1] Christian was chief justice of the Isle of Ely, based at Wisbech. Rather less humanitarian than his brother Fletcher Christian, the *Bounty* mutineer, he strongly advised that constables should carry pistols at all times (fortunately this advice was ignored) and firmly believed that the country needed a force of almost half a million armed policemen to keep order. His attitude towards sentencing was consistently severe. In 1819 he sentenced two young men to death by hanging for the theft of 21 shillings and the burglary of a home in Thorney; they were aged 20 and 24 respectively. Early in his career a superior had remarked that Christian was 'only fit to rule a copy book', and in 1823 a chronicler noted that Christian had 'died in the full vigour of his incapacity'.

them one woman, Sarah Hobbs – and the rest were to be jailed or sent to the penal colony of Botany Bay in Australia for between seven and fourteen years. Such severity was stunning and shocked many people in and around Ely. The judiciary eventually relented and commuted 19 of the death sentences to transportation to Botany Bay for life (not, in the eyes of many, a much better alternative). But the other sentences were carried out, and on 28 June 1816 Will Beamiss, George Crow, John Dennis, Isaac Harley and Thomas Smith were hanged. Their bodies were buried in St Mary's Churchyard in Ely, under a grave marker inscribed, 'May their awful fate be a warning to others'. The authorities' hope that this would serve as a deterrent to all future protesters was fulfilled. Some small-scale rioting continued on the Fens, but gradually the threat of violence from the peasants subsided – for the time being, at any rate.

But conditions for the workers and farm labourers did not improve much. There was little enough food and no luxuries; often the only real nutrition a family would see during a day was a bitter soup boiled up out of nettles. Housewives perfected the dubious art of making a kind of 'tea' by burning toast, scraping the charred bits into hot water and adding pepper (it may have looked like the real thing, but can't possibly have tasted like tea or, indeed, anything drinkable). So, in the 1840s, protesters once more railed against continuing poverty and the increased use of farm machinery, which put even more farm workers out of jobs. Countrywide, the unemployed and desperate men banded together under the banner of 'Captain Swing'. In fact no such person ever existed, but the mythical champion's followers were real; they set fire to hayricks and houses, stole sheep and smashed farm machinery. In the Fens most of the action took place in and around Willingham, Chatteris, March and Soham. Once again justice for those caught was merciless: two men were hanged for arson. The scale of the insurrection is reflected in the fact that in 1846 twelve men were charged with and convicted of sheep-stealing in just one day.

Not all attempts to better the common lot were violent. Both the Chartists and the Grand National Consolidated Trade Union had members on the Fens as early as the 1830s. In fact, the Fens was the site of an interesting early 'social experiment'. In 1838, the renowned socialist Robert Owen designed a 200-acre (80 hectares) co-operative at Manea. The motto of this 'Cambridgeshire

Community Number One' was 'Each For All'. It began with great expectations, but never reached the size Owen envisaged. Colonists lived in buildings they had erected and worked on the land in exchange for vouchers redeemable at the Co-op store. They organized both education and recreation. Unfortunately, the enterprise suffered from three major problems. First of all, it was woefully under-financed and managed to provide only a tiny portion of the facilities Owen had intended. The next obstacle came from within: the diverse characters working and running the commune could not even agree to disagree, and so internal dissension tore the place apart. Even that might have been a surmountable problem though, had it not been for the third hitch – drainage. The community never had the resources or the expertise to deal with the ever-present problems of flooding, and it had disappeared by 1851.

Others had more drastic solutions to the privations of life. After the agricultural depression of the nineteenth century over half a million farm labourers left England for the colonies. Many of these were men of the Fens and their families, hoping to escape poverty and starvation.

For those that stayed, life remained harsh. In the Fens proper (as opposed to the highlands and fen edges) at the end of the nineteenth century the Fenmen dug peat in summer, which they then burned all year long for heating and cooking. Also in summer they caught fish. As well as the plentiful species already mentioned, there was a strange breed of fresh-water cod called the burbot, which the Fenmen knew as the eel-pout, because it seemed half fish and half eel. Autumn was the time for netting plover, which were in abundance. In winter they stalked and shot wild duck and geese with large-bore muzzle-loaders mounted on punts. And many people lived with their floors under an inch or so of water all winter long; they put their boots on before they got out of bed and did not take them off again until they were back in bed. Often water that had invaded the house threatened to put out the fire – which was the only source of heat for warmth and for cooking – so the family would raise the hearth on stones to keep the precious fire safe from the encroaching waters.

Yet, despite living in such conditions, Fen folk were curiously hardy, some living to eighty or ninety, and having families of a dozen or more. They were inventive, too. Arthur Young, an agricul-

116

turalist and chronicler of the late 1800s, describes an interesting device used to get across the ice when the Fens froze: 'an ingenious and very simple tool ... A small frame that slides on four horse bones, the driver pushing himself forward with a pitchfork.' Often punt guns were mounted on these sledges, so they could be used for fowling (when the gun was fired, its recoil would propel the sledge backwards across the ice for yards).

At the end of the nineteenth century, the traditional Fen fowler was a dying breed. One of the last of them, Tom Harrison, lived in a hummock-shaped hut made of turf blocks. The walls, two feet thick, were plastered on the outside with clay to make them reasonably waterproof, and the structure was small and low – no more than the height of a man. It contained only Tom's essentials: a hard bed, a rough table, small fire for cooking, with a hole in the roof to let out the smoke. Most important of all would be the tools of his trade: his great punt gun, with its inch-and-a-quarter bore, and a smaller, double-barrelled muzzle-loader were hung high on the wall, well out of the reach of any encroaching water. He also had his 'dart', or fish-spear, and his trident-like glaive for spearing eels, as well as eel nets and baskets. He wore long leather boots which he

Glaive – used by Fenmen for spearing eels

hardly ever took off, and when he wasn't busy shooting and netting in the winter, he was cutting sedge and digging peat. Tom didn't actually own the land he lived on and worked, and he didn't care who did. People left him pretty much alone; after all, he was a fairly fearsome sight and, in any case, inhabited a part of the Fens that no one else really wanted anything to do with. He sold the eels and birds that he could not eat, and part of his payment was in laudanum, to alleviate the ague and rheumatism, both of which he had known for most of his life. Every season was hard, but winter was definitely the worst. Little had changed since Dugdale's *History of the Fens*, published in 1772, chronicled the annual challenge:

> In the winter time, when the ice is strong enough to hinder the passage of boats and yet not able to bear a man, the inhabitants upon the lands and banks within the Fens can have no help of food nor comfort for body or soul, no woman an aid in her travail, or partake of the Communion, or supply of any necessity, saving what those poor desolate places do afford, where there is no element of good – the air being for the most part cloudy and full of rotten harrs; the water putrid and muddy, yea, full of loathsome vermin; the earth spongy and boggy; and the fire noisome by the stink of smoky hassocks.

By the time the twentieth century began, a new type of Fen-dweller had taken over. He had emerged over two centuries or so as a result of the change from pastoral agriculture to arable. Many families continued to supplement their income by fowling, fishing and eeling, but employment was now largely on the land. There were two types of farm workers. The tied workers benefited from a regular wage as well as the use of a cottage owned by the farmer. This provided a degree of security, but it had drawbacks too. Tied workers often laboured under poor conditions, being, in some cases, the jacks-of-all-trades who were called on to perform the less attractive jobs on the farm; they had no choice but to carry out their duties as their employer demanded and had little chance to request improvements. In addition, although the tied cottage provided shelter for the worker and his family, it was also a source of concern – if a labourer lost his job, he lost his home as well. The other type of worker was the free man, rather like a freelance or contractor today. His main worry was lack of job security, as he worked on a job-to-job basis, with no guarantee of income. However, the free worker did tend to do the more specialised tasks and so often enjoyed better working conditions. When employed, he was also likely to receive a better rate of pay than the tied worker.

This new type of fen dweller was more dependent on the landowners than the old Breedlings, but he still had the same indomitable spirit that Charles Kingsley had described in his *Prose Idylls* (1873):

> It was a hard place to live in, the old Fen: a place wherein one heard of 'unexampled instances of longevity', for the same reason that one hears of them in savage tribes – that few lived to old age at all, save those iron constitutions which nothing could break down ... No one has ever seen a fen-bank break, without honouring the stern quiet temper which there is in these men, when the north-easter is howling above, the spring tide roaring outside, the brimming tide-way lapping up to the dyke-top, or flying over in sheets of spray; when round the one fatal thread which is trickling over the dyke – or worse, through some forgotten rat's hole in its side; hundreds of men are clustered, without tumult, without complaint, marshalled under their employers, fighting the brute powers of nature.

'A hard place to live in', just as it had always been. Many died young and the number living beyond 65 was half that of today. Illness was frequent, with little in the way of medical intervention; many families lived miles from the nearest doctor, who, in any case, often had little to offer against epidemics of measles, whooping cough, etc. The elderly and the young were at greatest risk, as we can see from the records of a school in Ely that had some 230 pupils on its register. In just two months in 1906 the following absences were recorded:

January 22nd: low attendance – whooping cough.
January 26th: 40 children ill.
February 5th: 50 children ill – whooping cough.
February 8th: only 137 children present ... through sickness and a terrible tempest and hailstorm at 2 pm.

The diet for a farm worker's family was plain, boring and not terribly nutritious. A typical meal was potatoes and swede and a large pastry roll (sometimes made with onions). If there was any meat to be had, it was the men who ate it, with the women and children getting a bit of gravy to go with their vegetables and roll. Sometimes there would be a pudding, which would be another stodgy affair.

The worker's cottage was very simple and often overcrowded.

Floors were covered with linoleum or coconut matting, sometimes rag rugs made out of old clothes. In winter the kitchen floor was usually covered with straw, as this meant less time spent cleaning up the ever-present mud tramped in from outside. The kitchen fire was fuelled with whatever was available – turf, old shoes, anything combustible – and summer days could be stifling, because that fire was the only source of heat for cooking and had to be kept going all year round.

Many of the men working on the farms were ploughmen or horsemen, for the horse was a major source of motive power for ploughing, drilling, harrowing, carting, etc. Horsemen both worked the horses and cared for them, earning approximately 30 shillings (£1.50) for a seven-day week (boys generally took up these duties at the age of 13). When necessary, the whole family was called in to help out – and schools were often closed at harvest time so that the children could work the fields too. Every able body would be involved with the gleaning after harvest, as gleaned grain could provide flour for the farm workers and their families: on a good day more than 25 lb (11 kg) could be gleaned.

In addition to helping out as required, children were expected to go to school, although attendance was somewhat haphazard. As well as illness and farm duties, the weather frequently kept children away from class. Another school record contains these entries:

29th January 1900: Bad weather and impassable droves lowered attendances.

13th January 1902: Icy weather lowered numbers from normal 140 to 47 in the morning.

3rd March 1909: Snow storm, six inches of snow. 50% absenteeism.

Schooling was thorough though. In addition to the Three Rs, subjects taught included science, history, geography, drawing, singing and needlework. An important and very practical part of the curriculum was gardening.

A school built in Benwick in 1872 was typical of those in Fenland towns and villages. It had three high-ceilinged classrooms of about 40 ft by 18 ft (12 m by 5.5 m) for up to 240 pupils. On one particularly full day the headmaster reported 'great difficulty experienced in accommodating 70 boys in eight desks'. Conditions were harsh;

there was only primitive heating, usually provided by one stove. A School Inspector at the turn of the century reported the temperature at one school as below 40° F (4° C) on seven days and below 45° F (7° C) on a further 32 days – it was not uncommon for the ink in the inkwells to freeze during such periods. And discipline was harsher still. Children would earn two 'stripes' on the hand for such crimes as impertinence, lateness, talking, idleness, fighting, inattention and even having dirty boots. Anyone perpetrating the same crime twice would collect four 'stripes'.

So far, the picture painted is a grim one, but there were respites. Recreation was, of necessity, largely home-made, but there were rivers to swim in and trees to climb. A favourite family treat was a trip to one of the local fairs. A farm wagon would be filled with hay and a basket of food, and the whole family would travel for up to two hours to enjoy the fun of the fair. And, of course, there was the skating, which was hugely popular. In his *Reminiscences of Fen and Mere* (1876), J.M. Heathcote describes a scene of enjoyment:

> The ice was good. The scenery of the Fen rivers, at all times beautiful, in the eyes of those who appreciate Dutch art, is peculiarly so in the winter. The mills, of varied form and colour, are conspicuously placed on the banks; cottages also ... with willows and trees denuded of leaves, make most picturesque groups; and then there are cattle standing by old hovels built by the owners. Boats, eel-trunks, frozen up in the ice, slackers all closed up and useless, little gunning-boats with their sprits lying on the bank, stacks of reed by the side of the river, groups of figures skating, some drawing sledges loaded with sedge – all these are objects of beauty and interest.

In 1900 the population of the Fens had increased to 239,000, with approximately 2.5 acres per person. The Breedling's way of life had given way to the new agricultural economy, but the Fen Tigers survived.

9. Fun on the Fens

It may have been a hard life on the Fens – never a land for lotus eaters – but there was fun to be had, and Fen folk were always determined to enjoy themselves when the opportunity offered. One great family favourite was quoits, and many inns and pubs had quoits grounds where the locals gathered to play, sometimes even for small prizes. Four Pins was another game often enjoyed in pubs; it was a form of skittles that was still being played in the early part of the twentieth century. A far less pleasant diversion, and one which hardly deserves the title of 'sport' was nevertheless a common practice on the Fens up until fairly modern times. Pinioned ducks would be released on a cordoned-off stretch of water, and dogs were then sent out to catch them.

The frozen rivers and meres gave birth to a game played across the world today: ice hockey. The early form of ice hockey, known as 'bandy', stemmed from a game called 'shinny' that was played on land with a ball (cat) and curved sticks (bandies); when the rivers froze, it was an obvious move to take the action on to the ice. Bandy was invented at Bury Fen, which hosted inter-village matches in the late eighteenth century and throughout the nineteenth. The team consisting of players from Bluntisham and Earith remained unbeaten for over a hundred years. By the time they were finally bested by the London Virginia Water Ice Club, the game was well on its way to the international ice hockey that is played today, having been introduced abroad by Fen skaters who attended skating matches in Norway, Sweden, Denmark, Holland and Germany.

Of Feasts and Fairs

The first festival of the year, and one which was particularly suited to the now predominantly arable Fens, was Plough Monday: the second Monday in January. This was obviously not a time when much ploughing (or any other important farm work) could be done, so the festival was presumably intended to improve magically the success of the crops to be planted in the spring. Plough boys, with blackened eyes and wearing their coats inside out, were set to the task of dragging a horse plough from door to door. These plough witches, as the boys were called, would call at each house demanding money. Although in most places it was a happy village event, accompanied by singing and dancing, in others it was somewhat more sinister, and some villages obviously took the ritual more seriously than others. It was not uncommon for a householder who refused to give money to the witches to find that a furrow had been ploughed in front of his house. Some crafty villagers heated coins in their hearths before the boys arrived and handed over the hot cash. In Ramsey, apparently, Plough Monday was seen as an opportunity to pay off old scores; what ensued was often pure and simple vandalism, with houses damaged or livestock allowed to escape. Interestingly, a song sung by the plough witches in Sawtry is very similar to a well known Christmas carol:

> I am a little ploughboy.
> My shoes are very thin.
> I have a little money box
> To put a penny in.
> If you haven't got a penny, a ha'penny will do.
> If you haven't got a ha'penny, God bless you.

Straw Bear Tuesday appears to be a ceremony unique to the Fens, particularly the area around Ramsey and Whittlesey. Seemingly less sinister, this followed on the heels of Plough Monday and made use of the same ploughboys. Now they were dressed from head to foot in straw. However, they were still after money as, in the guise of straw bears, they solicited alms. A man from Ramsey Mereside, who had been both a plough witch and a straw bear as a child, described the ceremony. The bear was fashioned of lengths of twisted straw which were wound round the young lads. The disguise was completed by securing two straw-bound sticks on their shoulders. The sticks joined together above the head forming a cone and the boys pretended to be fierce bears by walking on hands and knees groaning and growling fiercely.

It is very doubtful that these lads kept any of their takings from either the Monday or Tuesday, but it sounds as if they enjoyed themselves. The Straw Bear Festival still takes place annually at Whittlesey, although it is inevitably a somewhat tamer, more tourist-oriented event these days. The Festival is now a weekend of Morris dancing and folk music, complete with dancing straw bear.

The great Meres (now long since drained) used to be the site of many a feast, fair or picnic. Locals gathered there on public holidays, and there would be sideshows and other amusements, as well as stalls and vendors. A family could treat themselves to hot chestnuts, sausages, pork pies, doughnuts and cakes. The less abstemious could buy ale or a nip of gin to keep out the damp. At Whittlesey Mere, the greatest and last of these inland 'lakes', there was even a bandstand and musicians to keep the crowds entertained with marches, folk songs and jigs.

Some fairs got a bit out of hand. Upware had an annual entertainment called the Bustle, which was very popular with Cambridge undergraduates and people from surrounding villages, as well as the locals. The attractions included dancing, booths, skittles and 'prizes for various alcoholic feats'. It was perhaps these that led to trouble in 1862, when a fight broke out that ended up with several policemen being thrown into the river. (There is no record of any repercussions, so presumably it was all dismissed as good Fen fun.)

It wasn't just the local workers and their families who made good use of the Meres; they were a popular destination for the gentry too. In the early 1800s William Pierrepoint of Orton arranged an extravagant picnic on Whittlesey Mere for the Bishop of Peterborough and some of the luckier members of his clergy. They had melons with port for their first course, followed by venison, pasties, beef, mutton, duck and chicken; all this was rounded off with apples, cakes and tarts and plenty of wine.

Whittlesey Mere was everybody's favourite spot for a bit of outdoor fun, particularly in Victorian times: visitors could sail a pleasure boat, have a picnic, buy treats and souvenirs or watch punt gunners competing for the biggest 'bag' of the day. A sailing regatta was held every summer, and literally thousands of people turned up to take part and to watch (in 1847 approximately 2,000 people attended to see more than 50 boats compete). The lesser folk brought picnics, ladies and gentlemen dined 'al fresco', and ladies paraded in their best finery, making sure to be seen as much as to see. All the same, it didn't pay to forget the capricious Fen weather. The members of one sailing party were enjoying themselves hugely, admiring the boats on a fine summer's day, when an unfortunate and unexpected thunderstorm drenched them – ladies, finery and all. They had to bail out their boats, which were soon more than half full of water, and then to call off the rest of the day.

In winter, when the Mere froze, it was even better, because then the great Fen skaters took to the ice. A particularly cold winter in 1844 made for perfect skating conditions, and more than 6,000 people turned up to watch the Fen Tigers battle it out in speed races across the ice. Refreshments of all sorts were available, and there was even a band on the ice. It must have been a hard winter that year, for 6,000 spectators, complete with carriages, horses and sledges, plus the band and the purveyors of wines, beers and other temptations were not heavy enough to break the ice.

The Cradle of British Skating

Skating as a method of traversing the frozen rivers and swamps probably dates back to the Stone Age in northern Europe and Scandinavia. There is an Icelandic legend of Uller, the God of Winter, getting across the ice on the bones of animals. By the four-teenth century skating was very popular in Holland, both as a means of transport and a recreation. In England, there is evidence that Londoners were skating for fun in the twelfth century: William Fitzgerald, who had been clerk to the murdered Thomas à Becket, describes some skaters seen on the marshes north of London in 1180: 'Many young men play upon the yce [ice] ... Some tye [tie] bones to their feete, and under their heeles ... Some shoving them-selves by a little picked staffe, doe slide as swiftlie as a birdie flyeth in the aire, or an arrow out of a crosse-bow.'

It seems odd, but skating appears to have been slower arriving on the Fens. Given the difficulties Fenmen faced all year long getting across the swamps, it is hard to believe that they didn't come up with some means of making use of the frozen waters. But perhaps the remote and secluded nature of the Fens simply means that there are no early records of their use. Certainly, long before skating as such is reported fowlers had mastered the basic principle of sliding across the ice. They fixed sharpened animal bones to the bottom of

125

their punts, then by pushing with a pole or a long animal bone, they could make very good time across the ice. In fact, it is likely that Fenmen had been sliding across the ice for a long time, for primitive skates made of sharpened animals bones have been found throughout the area. An excellent selection of these can be seen at the Norris Museum in St Ives.

All sorts of theories abound about the advent of metal skates on the Fens. One takes us back to the eleventh century when the Norman Frenchmen building Ely Cathedral are said to have made good use of the local bounty by catching wildfowl. The Fenmen resented the foreigners raiding their larder and tried to chase them off, but the Frenchmen had some means of escaping across the ice so quickly that they evaded capture. When one of them was eventually ambushed and caught, the Fenmen discovered that he was wearing strips of iron fixed to the sole of his wooden shoes: skates.

Perhaps a more plausible, if less colourful, explanation is that a shipwrecked Dutchman ended up in Southery, where the villagers took him in and came to appreciate his skills as a blacksmith. Soon he was making skates for his new neighbours, using the methods he had learned in Holland. There is some evidence to back up this theory, as there is today a place called Catsholme Farm near Southery; this is believed to be a derivation of the name 'Schaatsholme'. 'Holme' means 'island' or raised dry ground in a marsh or river meadow and 'schaats' means skates.

It has also been suggested that the Dutch labourers who came over to work for Vermuyden on his great drainage schemes in the seventeenth century brought their 'schaats' with them. That seems very likely, and it may well be that this influenced the style of later Fen skates, but it is doubtful that the idea of devices for traversing the frozen waters would have come as any great to surprise to Fenmen at this late date.

Whatever its origins, skating was common throughout the Fens. Many of the meres and rivers froze solid in winter and became ideal rinks or racecourses (though skating was a means of getting around during the frozen winters, long before it developed into a competitive sport). The early skates were primitive, probably made from the leftover bones of sheep. Later Fenmen used metal pattens. But it was the coming of the Dutch 'schaat' that allowed them to achieve the terrific speeds of which they were so proud. The 'schaat' had a curl at the front, which the Fenmen cut off, leaving a curved front:

126

this is the form that became known as the 'fen runner'. The new style allowed skaters to achieve amazing speeds; even an average skater could cover a mile in 3½ to 4 minutes. But Fen skaters weren't just speed specialists. It was not at all unusual for a normal housewife or farmer to skate up to 35 miles – very handy for getting to and from the nearest market town, 15 or so miles away.

Fen skater. The men of the Fens were famous skaters, winning competitions at home and all over Europe.

There is no doubt that English speed skating originated on the Fens. The first recorded race, a 15-mile event, was held in 1763, and by 1820 organized racing was taking place all over the Fens. The most popular venue was Whittlesey Mere, but there were also matches elsewhere, including regular events at Crowland, Welney and Littleport. (As regular, that is to say, as the weather would allow: some winters saw no skating at all.) Local men soon became famous for their skating skills, consistently winning national championships, many of which were held on the Fens. These were not professional sportsmen – all made their living at some other Fen trade and could only practise their skills in slack periods (or indeed when travelling from place to place in the course of their work). Fortunately, those slack periods, for many a farm worker, coincided with the winter months when the rivers became ice rinks. Indeed, a harsh winter could put up to 3,000 labourers temporarily out of

127

work. Many men entered the races for a chance to win extra provisions for their families, or sometimes the money to buy food; prizes were typically a side of bacon or a pig's head, leg of mutton or loaves of bread. These events, called 'bread and meat' races, helped see many a family through a tough winter.

A typical match would begin at about two o'clock, weather permitting. (Always weather permitting. The racers could not be sure the event would take place until mere hours before the off, and in some years, no races were held all winter long, due to warm weather or, sometimes, just too much snow on the ice.) The crowds would begin to gather an hour or so before the event. Usually the course would be straight, with a barrel at each end, around which the men would turn at great speed, doing several laps of the course in each heat. As the competitors got ready, taking off bulky clothing and replacing it with more aerodynamic garb, the spectators crowded around the start and finish lines. Often skaters would have to go up and down the course before the race started to keep it clear of over-enthusiastic fans. The matches were usually run in heats of two until, finally, there were only two contenders left. That was the really exciting race of the day. By that time it would probably be starting to get dark, and often the weather would have changed, making the ice treacherous, with puddles or snowdrifts. But this was what the crowd had come to see – the last race between two Fen Tigers, battling against the weather, the cold, exhaustion and each other to claim the trophy.

The fame of the Fen skaters grew. Families of racers became well known all over England. Their members seemed to have had a penchant for strange nicknames, so we see William 'Turkey' Smart and 'Fish' Smart – though reputedly the best skater of them all was their brother James, who had no nickname at all. But there were plenty of others: 'Guttapercha' See, 'Chafer' Legge and 'Swearing Jack' Cooper among them. They performed amazing feats. The usual competitive distance was two miles, and as early as 1821 John Gittan (or perhaps Gittam) of Nordelph covered this distance in two minutes and 53 seconds, averaging over 41 miles per hour. In 1870 a race was staged between a skater and a train travelling from Littleport to Ely – a distance of four miles. Probably in fun, those who had put their money on the train cheated by throwing clinker (remnants of burnt coal from the engine's boiler) on to the ice to thwart the opposition. But it was

128

Today's Fenland has a vast array of fields and crops

Modern drainage pumps on the River Lark, controlled electronically

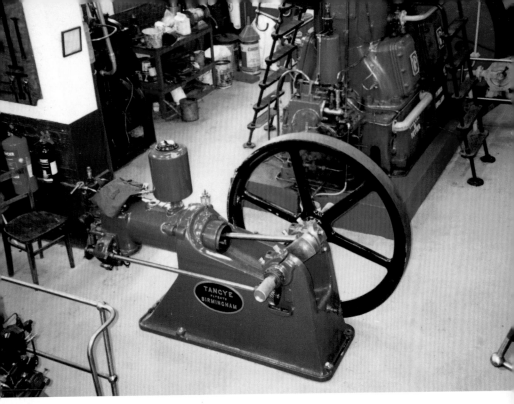

Reconditioned diesel pumps displayed at Prickwillow Drainage Museum

Swans and ducks enjoying the refuge at Welney Wildlife Reserv

One of the many butterflies to be seen at Welney Wildfowl and Wetlands Trust

Effigies or hexes were often hidden in houses to ward off evil. This one was found in the rafters of a house near Downham Market

Higgledy-piggledy house near Littleport, showing one of the effects of the shrinking peat

The old and new Holme Fen posts. The original was buried so that its top was at ground level in 1851. Both the original and the duplicate replacement now rise 13 feet above the ground

Like so many of the large old mills along the River Great Ouse, this one at Huntingdon has been converted into luxury flats

The land of the three-quarter sky. Sunset along the Great River Ouse

Denver Windmill – originally used to mill grain, now a tea shop and museum

Marsh roundwort, a typical Fen plant, grows in abundance at Welney Wildfowl and Wetlands Trust

The old sluice at Welmore Lake, built in 1935, photographed just before it was replaced by a new structure in 2000

Swans arrive from as far away as Siberia and Iceland to over-winter at Welney Wildlife Reserve

Sunset over Welney Wash

to no avail, as the skater finished a good half a minute ahead of the train.

Watching and supporting the skaters was something almost all Fen folk enjoyed, but what started as informal events soon developed into an organized sport. In 1879 the National Skating Association was formed, standardizing rules and enforcing regulations. It was at this time that a distinction was formally made between the amateur and professional skater; according to the NSA: 'An amateur is one who has never competed with or against a Professional for any prize, and has never taught, pursued, or assisted in the practice of athletic exercises as a means of obtaining a livelihood since 1st December 1879.' But the term 'professional' did not carry the same meaning as it does today. Whereas amateur skaters competed for trophies and medals, professionals vied for prizes, which could be anything from a sack of flour to a small purse of money collected from the crowd. Almost all Fen skaters, whether professional or amateur, made their livings as farm workers or labourers. Indeed it was often this work that gave them the strong physiques and seemingly unending stamina that made them skating champions. Many, such as the famous William 'Turkey' Smart, did drainage work (he developed his muscles as a 'clay man' digging trenches). Many a competitor would turn up at a race having already done several hours of heavy farm work or labouring and then skating miles to the event. He would then proceed to race, sometimes for miles, through numerous heats.

By the 1890s Fen skaters were taking part in international matches, both at home and abroad, and they often won. That was probably the heyday of skating on the Fens. The beginning of the twentieth century brought a series of mild winters that put paid to any racing; then along came the First World War, and no more racing took place until 1917. That year, the temperatures plummeted well below freezing and the *Peterborough Advertiser* of 10 February 1917 described the ice as a 'skaters' paradise', reporting that 'From early morning till late at night skaters are seen on the ice, and after office and shop hours crowds flock down there by moonlight'. The Fen folk had obviously missed their favourite winter pastime. Although the NSA had decreed that all matches should be suspended for the duration of the war, it conceded that it would be willing to allow races involving those in His Majesty's Forces, as well as those not old enough to be called up. In any case, the weather was just too perfect and many 'unofficial' local matches were held.

After that, the Fen folk had to do without skating for several more years. Until 1929 in fact, when, once again, it was skating weather, with ice up to ten inches thick in places. All the major races were held that year. Then came another spell of mild winters, followed by the Second World War, when, as previously, no official races were sanctioned.

As early as 1880 a newspaper reporter had observed, 'Given a good old-fashioned winter, the fenny men turn out with skates it may be seven years' rust upon them'. After the massive floods of 1947, though, the skates got even rustier. Improved drainage and other flood-prevention measures meant that the rivers ran more quickly and were deeper than before, and so were much less likely to freeze. In recent years, general global warming has played a part too. But the Fen Tigers, stubborn and persistent in this as in all things, have not let Fen skating die out entirely. On the odd occasions when the winter is cold enough, they temporarily flood sections of the Fens and get their skates out again.

Journey Through the Fens

Over the centuries people of all sorts have made their way to the Fens, from hermit monks to rebels to kings, but the years after the great drainage saw the start of a new arrival: the tourist. For, although the land is flat, it is far from boring. Ever-changing skies provide dramatic cloudscapes that alter from minute to minute (not for nothing is this known as the Land of the Three-quarter Sky). The sunrises and sunsets on the Fens alone are worth any effort made to get there. Adding to the appeal are miles of peaceful (or usually peaceful) rivers fringed by willows, with lazy sheep and cows nibbling at the river's edge. Swans sail gracefully along, confident kings of the river, regally ignoring the various ducks and other waterfowl. And the Fens have long provided a refuge and a home for all kinds of unusual flora and fauna.

The eighteenth century saw what could be described as the start of the tourist trade. In 1774 Lord Orford decided that it would be fun to take a party of his friends across the Fens in a fleet of nine boats. George Walpole, third Earl of Orford was, by all accounts, a

130

personable man, if somewhat eccentric, and a contemporary ascribes to him 'the easy, genuine air of a man of quality'. The grandson of the great Prime Minister, Sir Robert Walpole, the Earl was at various times Lord Lieutenant of Norfolk, Colonel of the Norfolk Militia, Lord of the Bedchamber and High Steward of King's Lynn and Yarmouth, to name but some of his titles. He could obviously afford the time and, indeed, the enormous expense of the expedition, and he is known to have been interested in agriculture, and this was probably what attracted him to this newly fertile part of the realm. He took along with him several friends, including his mistress, Martha Turk. He and his guests sailed (or were sometimes towed by horse) from Outwell to March, to Whittlesey Mere and on to Peterborough and Benwick, then along the Great and Little Ouse to Lakenheath. Like many tourists, they made scathing entries in their diaries about the locals. One wrote of Outwell: 'It is equally remarkable for the ugliness of the inhabitants as for the handsome-ness of the church – a disagreeable sallow complexion, broad flat nose, and wide mouth predominating among them.' Lord Orford was particularly uncomplimentary about the local women: 'Many very old women in Upwell, Outwell and March; the sex in general extremely ugly. The town populous. Crops of all kinds plentiful.' As the journey progressed, though, his opinion improved, and by the time they reached Ramsey he wrote: 'We found the sex much hand-somer, and the town better situated and built than any other we had seen in the Fens. The girls had many of them guido [he presum-ably meant 'good'] faces, with fair hair and good shapes, with expression, and life in their countenances: this we attributed to the mixture of French refugee blood settled here in the last century.'

It was a very well planned expedition. Some of the boats simply carried their provisions, others provided accommodation for those who prepared the meals and looked after the travellers – watermen, maids, cooks, and so on. The travellers generally slept on one of the other boats. Sometimes they visited inns ashore. These adventurers who were keen to see the strange land that was the Fens obviously had no inclination to rough it. They travelled by wind and horse power. (The horse in question, named the Hippopotamus, was treated well and had his own stabling on one of the smaller boats. Orford, who amused himself with the title of 'Admiral of the Fleet', often stopped the convoy when he noted that the animal was tiring.) With great foresight, Orford even took along a carpenter

131

whose duties included dismantling any bridges that stood in the way of the fleet and rebuilding them once they had passed.

The journey took three weeks and seems to have been enjoyed by all, including curious Fen inhabitants who turned out in droves to gawk (as Orford himself put it) at this extraordinary convoy of foreigners who had come in such great style to observe their flat land. It must be said that this particular pleasure trip to the Fens did not trigger an immediate tourist invasion. Nevertheless, once the age of the railways had become established, in Victorian times, day trips into the Fen countryside began to gain in popularity.

The End of an Era

As the draining of the Fens took an increasingly strong hold over the look and lie of the land, so more and more wetland gave way to fields of crops. One by one the meres disappeared, and the greatest was the last to go. The draining of Whittlesey Mere in 1851 was an enormous occasion, attracting visitors from all over and providing a good excuse for families to take time off from day-to-day survival to enjoy the great event. Hundreds came to watch, many bringing baskets, pails, buckets, whatever they could find to take home the vast numbers of fish that would be stranded and ready for the picking. They weren't disappointed: there were so many fish in the Mere that thousands were left gulping their last even after everyone had collected all they could manage.

Whittlesey covered a large area, although by the time it was drained it had already shrunk considerably. It was once 1¾ miles (2¾ km) long and 1½ miles (2½ km) across, covering 1,600 acres (650 hectares) in summer and over 3,000 (1,200 hectares) in winter. Needless to say, it took powerful pumps to get this water out, and they came from the Great Exhibition: 25-hp Appold centrifugal pumps which sucked the water from the Mere at 1,680 gallons (7.6 m^3) per minute. As the water level fell the spectators saw some amazing sights. Animal remains included the skulls of a wolf and a wild boar, as well as the skeleton of a killer whale. In the centre of the Mere was a prehistoric dugout canoe about 27 feet (8 m) long and made of oak; finely dressed Victorian ladies and gentlemen posed in front of and beside it for commemorative portraits. There were treasures too, the most important find being a silver incense boat, censer and chandelier which had been lost years previously on their way to Ramsey Abbey.

Finally the last of the great Meres was dry and used for growing crops. A contemporary writes in 1853 'the wind, which in the autumn of 1851 was curling the blue water of the lake ... was blowing in the same place over fields of yellow corn'.

An Odd Society

More and more people began to recognize the value of the Fens as a leisure destination. The sense of being slightly removed from the rest of the world, which always has and always will pervade the Fens, enhanced this appeal. It also led to some decidedly odd sorts exploiting the recreational possibilities of the area. One such interesting group of people formed the odd and quixotic Upware Republic Society in 1851. The area around Upware was a haven for Victorian naturalists, fishermen and shooting men, and the Society's members were almost entirely Cambridge undergraduates wishing briefly to escape academic life. They referred to themselves as a 'sporting republic' and had an elaborate system of government and rules of conduct. Headquarters was the *Lord Nelson* at Outwell, a hostelry better known as the 'Five Miles from Anywhere, No Hurry Inn'. The Society's record-keeping was sporadic, but it is known that members included students who later became well known as mathematicians, high church officials and MPs; Samuel Butler, author of *Erewhon*, was among them. More than 300 members visited the nerve centre at the *Five Miles from Anywhere, No Hurry Inn* before the Upware Republic Society disbanded in 1866. This pub still exists, serving food and drinks on the edge of the River Cam.

The appeal of the Fens for tourists continued to grow. Nowadays there is a thriving boating industry, and the area is particularly popular with fishermen and naturalists. Skaters are now rarely seen – victims of a warmer climate and, perhaps, professionalism in sport – and the great meres are only memories, but, despite these changes, in many ways the Fens have not changed greatly since Lord Orford and his friends explored the area in 1774. True, the farms are now mostly owned by syndicates, there are factories and modern shopping centres, and all the trappings of the twenty-first century are readily available. But it is not necessary to travel very far on the Fens to be transported back in time – to a world out of time. The skies are still huge, and the rivers still seem to flow thickly, even if for the most part they are well-maintained, scoured and regulated. The fishing is excellent and the wildlife, once the populated areas are left behind, abundant. Much that attracted the early visitors to the Land of the Three-quarter Sky remains.

10. Twentieth-century Fens

By the start of the twentieth century, Fenland was firmly established as a key agricultural area, producing potatoes, sugar-beet, wheat, oil-seed rape, carrots, celery and onions. These main crops were supplemented by market gardens specializing in berries and other fruits. Farming was the main occupation of most males over the age of ten, so the Fens was very much affected by fluctuations in market demand, as well as good and bad harvests and the changeable economy.

In earlier times, the isolated nature of the Fenland established it as a 'land out of time', and, except for major events happening on their doorstep, like the Viking invasion, matters that affected the rest of Britain hardly impinged on the Fen folk's way of life. As a result, innovation in farming methods and machinery was initially slower to take root in the Fens than elsewhere (although it is fair to say that the opposite is true today). Although the agricultural revolution had altered farming methods elsewhere, on the Fens much of the work was still done by hand. Whole families still worked the fields and lived on the farms – their lives a seasonal round of pulling peas, lifting potatoes, chopping beets and harvesting crops.

Fortunes fluctuated with the weather and national economic conditions; growers living near towns and railroads fared the best, especially those involved in horticulture. At the start of the twentieth century there had been years of poor harvests, and many farmers gave up completely or went bankrupt, and those who had worked on these farmers' lands for generations had a terrible struggle to survive. Indeed, some despaired entirely and left with their families for the colonies. Many a fen family started a new life in Canada, Australia or New Zealand.

135

World War I had a devastating effect on the Fens – as everywhere else in Britain – with fathers and sons going off to war, leaving wives and children to work the land and continue the day-to-day struggle to survive. Food was scarce, and the Fens played a key part in supplying the rest of the country. Ten years later came the Great Depression of 1929 to 1935, which saw many a family forced to return to the old ways of putting food on the table – at least there were still plenty of fish to be caught and birds to be netted or shot.

World War II

During World War II, the area played an even more important part in feeding the nation, and it is around about this time that the old Drowned Lands earned a new name – the Breadbasket of England. However, as well as the grain, fruit and vegetables so desperately needed throughout the country, the Fens produced one other, unique, crop. During the war, the military suffered a shortage of a vital part of their arsenal. The special, slow-burning charcoal used in shell-cases came from sources now under enemy rule. The charcoal was made from the wood of the alder-buckthorn, which grew in very few places in Britain. However, Wicken Fen had plenty of alder-buckthorn. Indeed the tree was over-running the place, threatening to destroy other important species growing there. So two problems were solved at once when the trees were harvested for military use.

If, as has been said, Britain was an 'unsinkable aircraft carrier' anchored off Europe, then a large part of its flight deck was in East Anglia, which had almost 100 airfields in 1939, increasing to over 750 by 1945. Admittedly, most of these were on the far edges of the Fens or just outside the area, but their presence had a major impact on Fen inhabitants.

There were two reasons for not siting airfields in the heart of the Fens. The first was the old problem of peat shrinkage – the land was considered too weak to support such large structures and runways. Far more important, though, was the fact that the area was put to much better use feeding the nation as it fought its war. The Fen fields were too valuable a source of food to be used any other way.

Nevertheless, there were a few airfields on the Fens or fen edge, including bases at Witchford and Mepal (near Ely), and Holme (near

Peterborough). But just outside the Fens was one of the best known of them all: RAF Wyton, headquarters of the famous Pathfinder Force, set up in 1942 to locate and mark targets for Britain's bombers, which by increasing the accuracy of bombing raids, contributed enormously to the eventual Allied victory. There were other airfields at Upwood, Warboys, Oakington and Downham Market.

Apart from appreciating the Fens' importance for food production, the government was also aware of the vulnerability of the area. Invaders over the centuries had used the Fenland rivers as pathways into the rest of England, and there was no reason to believe that the current enemies would not do the same thing, given the chance. Consequently, strategic defences against just such an invasion crisscrossed the Fens. And, although Fen fields were not suitable for use as air bases, they did look the part, and so made perfect decoy sites. All over the area sham airfields were set up to fool the enemy: fields and hedges were disguised to look like runways, or even industrial centres. One decoy site, around Burnt Fen, was made to look from the air like a major railway marshalling yard. Another subterfuge practised on the Fens was the training of soldiers in the gentle military art of deception. Many a Fen-dweller will tell of watching massive formations of men and tanks march and rumble through their village, and of their awe at the size of the force – until they realized it was the same very small troop marching down the street, doubling back on itself and marching through time and time again. This impressive piece of theatre was used extensively in Europe to make Allied strength appear much greater than it was, and by all accounts it was frequently successful.

A less significant but more personal effect of World War II on the Fens was to reinforce the North American connection that had begun with the emigration of large numbers of farm workers to Canada and the United States at the turn of the century. Now the area was full of American servicemen, many of whom took English brides home with them after the war. (It is interesting to note that the visiting servicemen sometimes mistook locals for Americans, because of their drawl – the same one that Fenmen had taken across the Atlantic with them earlier in the century.) There are still US air bases at Lakenheath and Mildenhall.

Of course, the war changed everything in Britain. The Fens did not escape. In the years after the conflict, tremendous farming subsidies

137

were on offer to encourage production. Farming became big business as syndicates bought up Fen farms; huge estates were formed, and large-scale production took over. Farming families who had survived the floods, the riots and everything else that Man and Nature had thrown at the Fens over the years became more prosperous than ever. It was a time of change all round, as finally, mechanization became the norm on Fen farms, and those working the land became fewer and less dependent on the landowners. Whereas at the beginning of the century, workers lived on the farms, many now had their own small homes, often driving to and from work and, in leisure hours, having a life separate from their jobs. Slowly, the Fens were making their way into the twentieth century.

Drainage

But, even by the end of the twentieth century, one thing remained the same. The Fens were still at constant risk from flooding. The introduction of diesel pumps, followed later by the even more efficient centrifugal electric engines, vastly improved the drainage of the land, enabling much greater quantities of water to be pumped off the fields and into the rivers and ditches to flow away to the sea. Unfortunately, though, the benefits conferred by the more powerful pumps were countered by the continuing problem of shrinkage of the soil. In some ways this was exacerbated by more efficient pumping, as more and more water was lost from the peat. Moreover, better, sturdier embankments on the rivers added to the problem, squeezing yet more moisture out of the soil. As the century continued, some farmers found that they had already reached the end of the line: their ploughs were beginning to strike the unproductive, buttery clay that lay beneath the rich peat.

Between 1930 and 1954 nearly £10 million (equivalent to £100 million today) was spent on continually raising and reinforcing the flood banks to counteract the constant shrinkage. But, although this gave better protection from floods, it still didn't solve the underlying problem, as the land continued to sink at a rate of up to 2 inches (50mm) per year. The Great Ouse Protection Scheme was proposed to try and stem the tide, but World War II put paid to those initial plans, and for another couple of decades little was done to improve conditions. Finally, in 1954, it was possible to put the scheme into effect. It took ten years to complete and cost more than £10 million, far and away the largest drainage project since the Great Adventure engineered by Vermuyden in the 1600s. Indeed, it was another bold adventure and arguably more effective than the Dutchman's efforts – certainly there were fewer nasty surprises upon completion.

The Scheme had many facets, but there were three major components. Over the years neglect had caused a tremendous build-up of silt and other debris in the main rivers, so 12 million cubic yards of material was dredged up and removed from the bed of the Relief Channel between Denver and Kings Lynn. Then both the Ten Mile River and the Ely Ouse were widened and deepened. And, lastly, another cut-off channel was formed: 29 miles (47 km) long, it ran from Denver into Suffolk.

After the Scheme was completed, various river improvement projects continued, including widening channels, protecting banks and repairing and replacing existing structures. And in the 1980s, Denver Sluice, the largest land drainage structure in Britain, underwent extensive refurbishment. Another major drainage project, prosaically named the Ouse Washes Flood Control Strategy, was undertaken in the 1990s, largely to rectify the increase since the 1970s in summer flooding on the Ouse Washes. A number of factors contributed to this, but the cyclical nature of flooding on the Fens was probably the major cause. Nowadays this is called 'climate change' and seen as a problem of global significance. But on the Fens it is an old story; the Fens have always had a mind of their own when it comes to weather and flood.

The Ouse Washes

Today's Fenmen live in a land that seems peaceful and regulated. With regimentally straight rivers and roads, acres of neat, well-tended fields, long stretches of flat, low land and empty skies, the Fens appear tamed. Indeed, many who live there now have no idea of the battle that is waged daily by Man against Nature. For the Fenland is a land wrested from Nature and re-shaped. No area exists that has not had its nature fundamentally altered by Man and his technology, but the Fens have been changed more than most places.

The clues are there, along the many long, straight roads through

139

the Fens. On one side of the road lie productive farmland, or homes or industrial areas; on the other, separated only by grassy banks, an unbending river flows to the sea. Nothing appears untoward. But the anomaly can be spotted from the vantage point of a bus or other high vehicle: that well-contained river is running at a level up to three feet (1m) higher than the fields on the opposite side of the road. As you pass through villages and towns, more clues appear. Every now and again there is a house with a strange-looking entrance. The doorstep juts out precariously three feet in mid-air, with much newer looking steps leading up to it; the ground-floor windows are seven feet above the ground. Over the years this house has risen higher and higher above the drained and shrinking Fenland soil. Further exploration reveals the enormous system of pumps, dykes and sluices that maintains the Fens. If left to its own devices for even a short while, this area would revert to the regularly flooded 'Half-Lands' of times past.

But one vast area of the Fens is a man-made reservoir: the Ouse Washes, created and maintained to act as a storage reservoir and safety valve for flood waters all along the Great Ouse and so protect the surrounding countryside. They are an engineering marvel – huge, complex and one of only a few of man's works that can be seen from space. Extending for 20 miles (32 km) and about 1,100 yards (1 km) across at the widest point, the Washes were created in the seventeenth century to keep floodwater off 72,000 acres (29,000 ha) of newly created agricultural land and allow major centres of civilization to grow and thrive. In the second phase of the project started by the Earl of Bedford, Vermuyden created a wash-land (land periodically flooded by overflow water from a river, stream, or from the sea) of around 4,700 acres (1,900 ha) between the Old Bedford River and the newly created New Bedford River. Here floodwater could collect, without inundating the surrounding farmland, and then be released safely into the rivers once the risk of flooding was past.

The current keeper of the Fens, in terms of flood defence, is the Environment Agency, which spends millions of pounds each year maintaining the mechanism and protecting farms, industry, towns and wildlife from flood. It is assisted by the Internal Drainage Boards, which take responsibility for the smaller rivers and drainages. Between them, they carry out a great deal more work on the Fens than is apparent. Sluices and pumping stations are

140

constantly maintained and upgraded. Recently, the Environment Agency completed an £8 million project to improve the Ouse Washes, which included replacing the old sluice at Welmore Lake in Norfolk. This sluice is the only means of removing water from the Ouse Washes into the tidal Hundred Foot River, and thence into the sea. Here, 12 miles (20 km) south of King's Lynn, the River Delph and the Tidal River Ouse meet. The sluice holds back waters stored on the Washes during a flood and, once the peak flood has passed, allows them to flow through and rejoin the Hundred Foot River and so to the sea. But the sea is the other enemy, and the structure must also keep the salt water of the tidal river off the Washes, lest it devastate valuable crops and render the surrounding land unsuitable for farming for some years to come.

The new sluice at Welmore Lake, which cost more than £5 million and took two years to build, can discharge up to 50% more water through its triple gates than its immediate predecessor. It is certainly a far cry from the first structure built in 1756; that was basically an embankment to hold in the waters during a flood – all very well up to a point, but when the water needed letting out to the sea, the barrier had to be broken down and then built up again afterwards.

The Ouse Washes Control Strategy is just a recent example of the continual maintenance and improvement that are essential to maintaining the Fens as they exist today. The Environment Agency has also put in place a multi-million pound automated Flood Warning System to help minimize the damage caused by floods. But, despite all these improvements, there was considerable flooding at the end of the twentieth-century – good old 'climate change' at work again! The first of several annual floods was in 1998, and it has to be said that it took everyone by surprise. At Easter that year, the peak water level in the Washes rose to 14 feet (4.3 m) above sea level. This meant that the flood control mechanisms were called on to store some 60 million cubic metres of water above the surrounding ground level – and, since that ground level is already about one metre *below* sea level, the enormity of the problem is obvious. All the flood defences that had been built and improved over the years were called upon, and it is to Man's credit that the damage to surrounding land was minimal. The floods of 1947 were not to be repeated – this time.

What this really shows in a rather dramatic way is that the Fens only survive as they are today because of constant vigilance. It really is hard work keeping Nature at bay. Expensive work, too. The Environment Agency announced in March 2001 that it intended to spend nearly £7m on flood defences in the Great Ouse Valley alone in the coming year. That didn't even include any great new schemes – the funds were earmarked solely for essential improvements of existing defences and systems to warn residents of the inevitable floods. The struggle goes on.

11. Towns and Cities

As a predominantly agricultural area, the Fens do not have a huge urban population. Nevertheless, there are several large towns, and these have largely grown from the market towns and ports that were distribution centres for Fen produce. Before drainage, market towns were the places to trade fish, eels, wildfowl and livestock. Later, when drainage allowed the area's rich soils to be exploited, the towns became markets for arable crops. The same commodities were shipped out through the ports, which also imported exotic goods from abroad and, via the Fenland rivers, distributed them throughout England.

Some of the towns described here are not, strictly speaking, on the Fens. Important places such as Cambridge are just outside the geographical area but have played an important role in the story of the Fens. There were a number of prosperous Fenland towns during the thirteenth and fourteenth centuries, many benefiting from the thriving wool trade. (Some Fenland towns were then amongst the richest in England). This trade later declined, but in the seventeenth century the draining of the Fens led to another period of prosperity.

The lives of the town folk were very different from those of their rural cousins, being perhaps more influenced by politics and country-wide movements. The history of the towns of the Fens thus reflects both local and national events.

Bury St Edmunds

This town lies strictly outside the boundaries of the Fens, but it played an important part in the Fenland's early history. Until the

Reformation it was a major religious centre. Its original church was founded in the seventh century by Sigebert , the first Christian king of East Anglia, in what was then called Bedricsworth. In about 870, Edmund, the last king of East Anglia, was killed by the Vikings. His body was later discovered to be uncorrupted, and in *c.* 903 it was moved to the church at Bedricsworth. In 925 King Athelstan of England founded a monastery to care for St Edmund's shrine, which became a famous destination for pilgrims from England and the Continent, and as a result the town became known as Bury St Edmunds. In 1020 King Cnut had the church rebuilt in stone, the monastery was reformed under the Benedictine Rule, and the surrounding settlement became a thriving market town. Although the medieval town was controlled by the Abbey, it survived the closure of the Abbey in 1539.

Bury St Edmunds had a heyday in the eighteenth century as a result of an increase in trade that was partly due to improvements made to the navigation of the River Ouse at the end of the seventeenth century. In addition to being a commercial centre, it became a fashionable centre for aristocracy and landed gentry, where they attended assemblies and went to the theatre. The Bury Fair held over several days in September attracted people from all round.

Bury continued to prosper throughout Victorian times, but the agricultural slump at the end of the nineteenth century hit it pretty hard. Trade in the town did not really improve until World War II, when the renewed importance of agriculture in the area once again gave the town a high profile.

Cambridge

Cambridge is now recognized as one of the UK's most significant university towns, but it was there for at least thirteen centuries before the arrival of the scholars. The earliest evidence of occupation comes from the Iron Age, when people from what is now Belgium settled there. Traces of their settlement have been excavated on Castle Hill, and it is likely that they were still there when the Romans came in the early part of the first century AD.

The Romans would have recognized the strategic importance of the area, situated as it was at the crossroads of the two major thoroughfares, Worstead (or Worsted) Street and Akeman Street, from Ermine Street to Littleport. There were other important Roman roads in the area – the Via Devana, from Colchester to Godmanchester, and Ermine Street, which linked London to Lincoln and the north. Additionally, the River Cam, although shallow in places, could take men and goods from East Anglia through to the sea at King's Lynn. The Romans built a bridge here and a small but significant town called Duroliponte on the west bank of the river. The Anglo Saxons, too, were aware of the value of the site, and in 875 they built another bridge over the river that they called the Granta. The town came to be known as Grantebrych (bridge over the Granta); by the twelfth century the name had evolved into Cantebrych, and by the fourteenth century it was recorded as Cambrugge (it wasn't until the seventeenth century that the river became universally known as the Cam).

In the twelfth century the Normans destroyed part of the Saxon settlement when they built a castle on the right bank of the river. From there they carried out a profitable river trade along the Cam to the Wash ports. As well as the castle, in 1107 they built the Church of the Holy Sepulchre, the oldest of four round churches in England.

Cambridge has several times been devastated by fire, and most of it was destroyed by a blaze in 1174, but the town soon recovered and continued to prosper. It is interesting to note that even here, several miles from the Fen edge, flooding was a problem; many medieval houses were built on small gravel ridges to avoid it.

By the end of the thirteenth century there were fifteen churches, two hospitals, a priory, a nunnery and four or five orders of friars in Cambridge. A significant contributor to the prosperity of the town in these times was the establishment of the Stourbridge Fair. This was held on the meadows north of the town each September and became one of the greatest trade marts of northern Europe. The Fair remained important for centuries, drawing traders, customers and visitors from England and the continent. Daniel Defoe visited in 1723 and described it as the greatest fair in the world, with goods from all over England and the continent displayed in booths that were arranged in rows like streets. Colourful parades opened the event each year, with great pomp and pageant, and hundreds of people came from London by coach to take part, the first such coach arriving in 1605. By the time Defoe visited in the eighteenth century, at least 50 coaches made their way from the capital, along with many hundreds of wagons full of goods and people. A guide-book of 1814 describes the produce on sale: 'supplied in the most abundant manner with every article of provision: the quantities that are exposed for sale are sometimes astonishing, and its quality is in general excellent … Great quantities of fruit are brought, in their season, from Ely and the villages … insomuch that, though very little fruit is grown in the town, no place in the world can be more plentifully supplied with it.'

So Cambridge was a thriving trade centre long before it had any scholastic connection. The scholars arrived early in the thirteenth century from Oxford, which was already established as a seat of learning. The legend is that in 1209 an Oxford townswoman was killed under mysterious circumstances; suspicion fell on some of the students, who immediately escaped the town. However, the mayor and burgesses were not willing to leave it at that, and they took other students as hostages. When this failed to rout out the suspected murderers, King John gave the authorities leave to execute the hostages. Not surprisingly, this ruthless attitude put the wind up several of the students who fled the town. Some went to Reading, some to Paris and others ended up in Cambridge.

The early students were very young, usually only 14 or 15, and were initially taught by clerks in holy orders. There were many reli-gious houses in Cambridge including Dominicans, Franciscans, Carmelites and, later, Augustinians. The first college with a formal constitution was Peterhouse, founded by the Bishop of Ely in 1280, followed by Michaelhouse in 1324 and King's Hall in 1337 (the last two were later amalgamated to form Trinity). King's Hall was the first college to house students as well as fellows; before this, students lived in rooms and boarding houses throughout the town – as, indeed, most continued to do for some time.

The relationship between the colleges and the townspeople was turbulent for many centuries. Henry Gunning, in his *Reminiscences of Cambridge*; wrote of eighteenth century undergraduates: 'To me (who have a perfect remembrance of all its horrible discomforts) it seems surprising that any family should have resided at Cambridge who could live anywhere else. The undergraduates when encoun-tered in our dark streets were scarcely less ferocious than the members of the "Mohock and Sweating Clubs".' And Lord Byron, who attended Trinity College from 1805 to 1808, referred to Cambridge as 'the dark asylum of a vandal race'.

Despite the coming of the scholars, Cambridge continued to be a market town, and by and large a prosperous one, although it did not escape the ravages of plague that decimated so many towns in England during the thirteenth and fourteenth centuries; in 1348 the Black Death killed almost all living in the vicinity of the castle, and by 1377 the population had fallen to 3,000. Then, in 1381 the Peasant's Revolt resulted in the burning of the books and charters of Corpus and other colleges. Houses and property belonging to the college burgesses were sacked. In 1385, yet another fire destroyed more than 100 houses.

Major events shaping the future of the town occurred in the seventeenth century. The first of these was the Civil War. Oliver Cromwell already had an association with Cambridge. Born not far away in Huntingdon, he had attended Sidney Sussex College, and in 1640 he was one of the town's MPs. When the Civil War began in 1642 he became another in a long line of military commanders to appreciate the strategic importance of Cambridge, situated on major roads between East Anglia, London and the Midlands. The town became the headquarters of the Eastern Counties Association, which was formed to defend East Anglia against the Royalists, and its defences were improved by strengthening the castle (the burgesses of Clare College were powerless to prevent Cromwell from confiscating materials meant for a new college building and using them for this purpose). Other preparations included destroying all bridges but one, so as to deny the Royalists access to the town, and the building of barracks for 300 men. In February of 1643, when it looked as if the royal army was about to attack, Cromwell raised a force of 30,000 men; the threat passed, but 1,000 of these soldiers stayed on in Cambridge. Needless to say, teaching was seriously disrupted, and the townspeople lived in a state of constant upheaval and fear. Masters, officials and students who were deemed anti-Puritan were expelled or sent to jail, and several of the churches suffered great damage when 'papist' statues, furniture and decorations were removed or destroyed.

The Restoration of the monarchy under Charles II brought its own havoc. Ejected officials and Masters returned, looking to take back their positions, and Quakers and Puritans were persecuted. In 1660 there were 67 members of the Society of Friends in jail. It was quite some time before the town regained its equilibrium.

The other main seventeenth century influence was also a key event

147

in the history of the Fens. The Great Drainage Scheme, headed by the Earl of Bedford and his Adventurers, might be thought to have had little effect on Cambridge, which lay outside the Fens. But Cambridge had long relied on the Cam and the rivers of the Fens as its supply routes for food, building materials and produce of all sorts. The fear was that the drainage would cause river levels to fall, so that boats and barges would no longer be able to reach the town. Indeed, the fear was to some degree justified, for the drainage did have an enormous effect on the Fen river system. A contemporary representative of the University complained: 'Whereas of old ships from Newcastle were wont to make 18 voyages in the year to Cambridge, with sea coal, now, since the block of the stream at Denver and the diversion of its waters to Earith, they can make but 10 or 12, whereby the price of fuel hath increased by half.' Opposition to the drainage works continued into the eighteenth and nineteenth centuries, but the town managed to maintain its position as a trading centre for all sorts of produce, including butter, corn-malt and fish.

At the beginning of the nineteenth century Cambridge's population was just under 10,000, approximately 600 of whom were undergraduates. The century saw a great deal of progress and change. The first train arrived in 1845. At the insistence of University officials the station had been sited a good way from the town centre, as it was felt that the ease of travel and escape from academia would encourage unscholarly behaviour among the students. Nevertheless, the advent of rail travel contributed to the town's growth. By the middle of the 1800s the number of undergraduates had increased to approximately 1,600, and by 1905 the town's population reached over 38,000 (if outlying districts such as Chesterton are included, the number increases to some 53,000). Perhaps the University officials were right to fear for the morals of their students, although it is doubtful that the railway was to blame; in 1906 when England and Wales averaged one pub for every 230 people, Cambridge had one for every 138!

Male domination of the University began to be threatened by the opening of the first women's college, Girton, in 1869. This was followed by Newnham in 1871 and Sidgwick Hall in 1880. Progress on this front was slow, however. Not until 1921 were women awarded degrees, and only in 1926 did they gain the right to be faculty members and fill teaching posts. Finally, in 1946, women were admitted to full membership of the University.

World War I affected Cambridge badly. As more and more men were called to the trenches, the number of undergraduates was cut by half, and thousands of soldiers were billeted or camped in the town. By 1916, 2,000 officers were quartered in the colleges, at a time when the undergraduates living there numbered only 575. However, the end of the war saw the introduction of scholarships and grants for ex-service men, and this quickly replenished the student population. By 1920 there were 5,733 students in Cambridge.

World War II had less effect; some undergraduates managed to get their call-up deferred, and 2,000 students were evacuated to Cambridge from the London School of Economics and from London University's Bedford College. It did, however, change the nature of the town, as several Government departments were located in the colleges, and a great deal of secret war work was carried out there.

In the post-war years the area around Cambridge became the most rapidly growing in England, and by 1961 the population exceeded previous estimates for 1971. A key reason was the emergence of Cambridge as a major centre of scientific research. The story of a well-known commercial name that originated in Cambridge illustrates the effect the existence of the University has had on modern industry in and around the town. In the 1880s instruments used by medical science students were mainly imported from Germany. Sir Michael Foster, Professor of Physiology, saw in this a business opportunity, and with two ex-pupils, Dew Smith and Francis Balfour, as partners, set out to make medical instruments. They engaged a skilled mechanic to produce their wares, and became very successful as the Cambridge Scientific Instrument Company. The mechanic's son set up his own similar business in 1896, with his father as a partner; a quarter of a century later this firm branched out into making wirelesses as well as medical instruments. The father was W.T. Pye, the son W.G. Pye, and the company was the internationally respected Pye Electronics, making radios, televisions, broadcasting networks, etc. Many other firms have since had a similar genesis, and it is this symbiosis between town and gown that underlies today's famous Silicon Fen.

Today technology, commerce, academia and the arts all flourish in Cambridge. Two million tourists visit each year. No doubt most come to see the colleges attended by well-known figures, among them Sir Isaac Newton, Thomas Grey, William Wordsworth, Lord Byron, Samuel Taylor Coleridge, John Milton, Alfred Lord Tennyson, William Pitt and Lord Palmerston. However, just as it was long before the scholars came to town, Cambridge is still a prosperous trading centre. The goods may have progressed from corn to computers, but the town remains a centre of international importance.

Ely

Ely may have existed as a small market town before the coming of the Church in the seventh century, but there is little archaeological evidence. It was not a key area during Roman times, although the Roman-built Akeman Street did run through the area that is now Ely on its journey from Cambridge to Littleport. As we know, the Fens were in a pretty soggy state after the Romans left, so it is likely that the early Anglo-Saxons took advantage of the island in the midst of the swamps. A late Anglo-Saxon pagan cemetery, found about a mile south of what is now Ely, belonged to a village called Cratendune. It is unlikely that anyone inhabited what is now Ely before St Etheldreda founded her monastery. Therefore, the city's history effectively begins at this point.

In 870 the monastery that St Etheldreda founded – a double monastery that housed both monks and nuns – was destroyed by the Vikings; it was refounded a hundred years later as a men-only Benedictine abbey. The changing fortunes of the Church are integral to Ely's tale, but another strand running throughout the city's history relates to its geographical position. The Isle of Ely stands above what were for centuries the swamps and marshes of the Fens, an isolated place with its own natural defences. Consequently, it has often been the home of rebels and the scene of insurrection and defiance. Probably the best-known example of this is the tale of Hereward the Wake's last stand against the Normans at Ely, exemplifying Anglo-Saxon resolve. But it is interesting to note that, although the monks betrayed Hereward and his rebels, William the Conqueror nevertheless imposed a stiff penalty on them: a £1,000 fine. That was an enormous amount of money in the eleventh century, and the monks were forced to melt down and sell almost all the gold and silver statues and decorations in the Church. It is perhaps evidence of the power and wealth of the Church on the Fens at that time that only twenty years later the Domesday Book recorded Ely as the richest monastery in England, with a gross yearly income of £768 17s 3d.

The monastery continued to thrive, owning great chunks of the Fenland around Ely and profiting from rents, taxes and tributes. In 1109 its abbey became a cathedral of a new diocese. The monks contributed to the life of the town around them by providing education for local children. A law was enacted in 1215 making it obligatory for cathedrals to provide a grammar school, but Ely's King's School had already been founded in 970 (Edward the Confessor was educated in the cloister school there). The townsfolk also benefited from the monks' skill as healers – although they were probably happy not to undergo the regular 'leechings' that the monks were subjected to at the time (blood-letting was thought to be very beneficial, and so each monk was 'bled' every seven weeks). The Church did a lot to maintain its great farm estates, too. Roads and bridges were built – the road that today runs from Ely to Stuntney and Soham was built on a causeway originally made across the Fens by the monks.

The next great siege at Ely, taking advantage of its isolated situation in the middle of the waterlogged Fens, involved Nigel, Bishop of Ely from 1133 to 1169, who opposed King Stephen. Once again, the insurrection was ultimately unsuccessful. Nothing remains today of the castle Nigel built at Ely.

The dissolution of the Monasteries in 1536 and 1539 affected Ely less than many other abbeys, perhaps partly because the Bishop of Ely, Bishop Goodrich, was an ardent reformer who supported Henry VIII in his fight against Rome. The monastery was dissolved, but the cathedral survived, and it wasn't until 1541 that Bishop Goodrich ordered 'that all Images, Relics, Shrines, etc., be so totally demolished and obliterated that no remains or memory be found of them' (it is likely that this was when the carvings in the Lady Chapel were defaced). The church personnel survived relatively unscathed – the monastery's last prior became the cathedral's first dean, and three of its eight canons were former monks, as were six of the eight new minor canons. Bishop Goodrich himself was eventually buried in the cathedral.

Oliver Cromwell's connection with Ely is worth looking at. He moved to Ely from nearby St Ives in 1638, and during his time in Ely he was the MP for Cambridge. It was in this capacity that he opposed the Earl of Bedford's and his Adventurers' attempt to claim land on the Fens as a reward for attempting to drain the area (the fact that all the Adventurers except the Earl went bankrupt tends to indicate Cromwell's success).

The Civil War began in 1642, four years after Cromwell came to Ely. Services in the cathedral continued unaltered until 1644, when Cromwell, in his capacity as Governor of Ely, wrote to the Reverend Hitch demanding that he 'forbear altogether the choir service, so unedifying and offensive, lest the soldiers should in any tumultuary or disorderly way attempt the reformation of the cathedral church'. The threat was clear, but, either in defiance or in ignorance of Cromwell's power, Hitch ignored it and carried on with his services as usual. Cromwell then paid a visit to the cathedral, accompanied by several of his armed men, and ordered the Reverend Hitch and his underlings to leave the cathedral. When they refused, Cromwell demanded: 'Leave off your fooling, and come down, Sir.' It was probably the armed men behind Cromwell rather than his words that caused the clergyman to capitulate. When all had left, Cromwell locked the front door of the cathedral and kept the key; it remained closed for the next 17 years.

Like so many before him, Cromwell was aware of the strategic importance of Ely, and he planned to conduct the defence of Cambridgeshire from the city in the event of Royalist attack. (The plans were never fully implemented – although in 1645 the Royalists did get as far as Huntingdon, only a few miles away, and several prominent Parliamentarians took refuge in Ely.) He is quoted as saying, 'I will make the Isle of Ely the strongest place in the world' and 'a place for God to dwell in'. He finally left Ely for London in 1646.

When Daniel Defoe visited Ely in 1724 he had surprisingly little to say about the town, although he was surprised at the state of disrepair:

The town, when the minster, so they call it is described, everything remarkable is said that there is room to say; and of the minster that is the most remarkable thing that I could hear, namely, that some of it is so antient, totters so much with every gust of wind, looks so like decay, and seems so near it, that when ever it does fall, all that

152

'tis likely will be thought strange in it, will be that it did not fall a hundred years sooner.

In 1750 Mr Essex, who was architect to several Cambridge colleges, was called in to survey the situation. He found much that needed maintenance and improvement. Over the next few years, sufficient repairs were carried out to secure the future of the cathedral.

Ely's role as a strategic stronghold re-emerged during the Napoleonic Wars of the late eighteenth and early nineteenth centuries. If Napoleon had invaded England, the intention was to use Ely as a place of refuge for important members of the royal family, politicians and other dignitaries.

The Napoleonic invasion never happened, but, shortly after the Battle of Waterloo, Ely came under attack from an unexpected source. The men of Littleport and the surrounding area marched on the city in 1816; some of them were men who had returned from the war only to find their families living in poverty. The Littleport rioters sacked several houses, inns and hostelries in Ely before being overwhelmed by troops and sentenced to hanging or transportation or prison. This was indeed a period of general unrest. William Cobbett, the political writer, was imprisoned in Ely for two years, as a result of a mutiny among the local militia. This was put down by four squadrons of German cavalry stationed at Bury, and Cobbett commented scornfully about it in his publication the *Weekly Register* and was fined £1,000 as well as being sentenced to jail.

The coming of the railway benefited the residents of Ely. In 1845 the main line from London to Norwich, via Cambridge and Ely, was opened. This was followed a year later by the line to March and Peterborough, and in 1847 by the route from Ely to King's Lynn. Up until this time by far the most efficient means of travel in the area was by river. In 1753 a passenger and goods boat left Cambridge for Ely every Tuesday and Friday, taking six hours for the twenty-mile journey, and returning the next day. Trains offered a great improvement on such journey times, making Ely more accessible than it had ever been. The resultant increase in Ely's population, from 3,948 in 1801 to 8,640 in 1891, demonstrates how this benefited the town.

The name Ely may derive from the Old English *Ēlgē* or *Ēlēg* ('eel district' or 'eel island'), and certainly eels played a major part in the

153

economy of the area. (Another suggestion is that the name comes from the Welsh *helyg*, 'willow'; there are a great many willow trees in and around Ely, and they too were once of economic significance.) At all events, for most of the city's history agriculture and natural resources have been the key to the local economy. The sugar beet factory which opened in 1925 provided much work until its closure in the late 1980s. Locally grown sugar beets are now processed at Wissington, near Downham Market, the largest such refinery in Europe.

World War II saw the Isle of Ely once again providing a safe haven, when it became a 'reception area' for children evacuated from London. Evacuees included pupils from a girls' grammar school, the Central Foundation School of London and the Jewish Free School for boys and girls. But many famous people have lived in or visited Ely over the years, including King Cnut, Daniel Defoe, Christopher Wren, the Prince Regent, Oliver Cromwell and various kings of England. Today, the city draws thousands of visitors each year, many of them to see its magnificent cathedral; tourism has become an important industry in this town which was once the haven of rebels. More than any other town or city on the Fens, the history of Ely has been, and continues to be, the history of the great church which shaped it.

King's Lynn

King's Lynn has always been an important port, linking the Fens with other English ports as well as those of northern Europe. It lies at the convergence of road, river and sea routes, and its connection to the fertile Fens, to Norfolk and the East Midlands, plus the ports of Europe, has made it a prosperous trading centre over the years.

Since the word 'Lynn' derives from the Celtic *llyn*, a pool or stretch of water, it would seem that this area has been inhabited since at least Celtic times. The earliest settlement was probably in South Lynn, and there may well have been a considerable population living in the area during the Anglo-Saxon period. The town was officially established in 1095, when Herbert de Losinga, Bishop of Norwich, was granted the charter for a market there. This may have come about as a result of requests from traders who were tenants on his nearby manor at Gaywood. The town that sprang up as a result became known as Bishop's Lynn (the name changed after the Dissolution of the Monasteries, when Henry VIII took over the church's assets).

The geographical layout of the area was very different in those days. The River Ouse and the River Nene then flowed to the sea at Wisbech. Due to the opening of the old Roman channel and excessive silting at Wisbech, the Ouse changed its course in favour of an outfall at Lynn. However, even before this, when only a few small streams flowed into the Lynn inlet, the town was still one of the richest ports in England; the change of the course of the Ouse only increased its prosperity.

Goods of all sorts went through Lynn. Exports were mainly agricultural commodities, especially wool. Imports included cloth from Flanders, wine from France, fish from Norway and timber and furs from the Baltic. In addition there was a thriving salt-producing industry, which would have attracted many traders.

By the time Henry VIII appropriated the Bishop's assets the boom had died down somewhat, and London had taken over as the key international port. Nevertheless, Lynn was still an important port, and it continued to prosper on river and coastal trade into the nineteenth century. Particularly important were corn, which was brought downriver and then shipped out to London, and coal, which came in from Newcastle.

In the mid-nineteenth century the coming of the railways inevitably meant a downturn in King's Lynn's fortunes, although it continued to be an international harbour and the base for a fishing fleet. Today the port handles timber from Scandinavia and Russia, as well as liquid bulk cargoes and coal, while the town still benefits from its location next to the Fens and is a centre for fertilizer production, canning, flour-milling and food processing. Other industries include shipbuilding, metalworking and light engineering.

The London 'overspill' of the 1950s and 1960s increased the population, so that today it stands at approximately 38,000. Despite modernization, the flavour of the ancient sea port remains in parts. Tourists come to see the home of such famous seamen as Admiral Nelson, who was born at Burnham Thorpe, and Captain George Vancouver, who sailed with Captain Cook and later charted the North American north-west coast. To these names can be added Captain John Smith, who served as an apprentice in King's Lynn; Captain Smith famously befriended Pocahontas who married John

155

Rolfe, coincidentally also born near King's Lynn. Another historical man of Lynn was Sir Robert Walpole, who built nearby Houghton Hall and served as the town's MP.

Peterborough

Like many other Fenland towns, Peterborough began as a market town and prospered as such for many years before it gained renown as a home of one of the highly influential Fen abbeys. The site was first inhabited c. 4000–3000BC, when the first farmers arrived. In many ways it is ideally located, being on the edge of the marshes, and therefore enjoying easy access to the undoubted bounty of the Fens, whilst being situated on dry land itself. There was plenty to be gleaned from the swamps, and abundant grasses, fish and fowl were available without the inconvenience of having to live in the marshes. The attraction of the area and the benefits of its situation are best summed up by Hugh Candidus, who wrote the first history of Peterborough:

> Situate in the region of Grywas, because this same fen begins there on the eastern side, extending for 60 miles or more. This same is very valuable to men because there are obtained in abundance all things needed for them that dwell thereby, logs and stubble for kindling, hay for the feeding of their beasts, thatch for the roofing of their house, and many other things of use and profit, and moreover it is very full of fish and fowl. These are divers rivers and many other waters there, and moreover great fishponds. In all these things that district is very rich. So this Burch is built in a fair spot, and a goodly, because on the one side it is rich in fenland, and in goodly waters, and on the other it has abundance of ploughlands and woodlands, with many fertile meads and pastures.

Modern estate agents stress the importance of location, and there is no doubt that the area around Peterborough scores well on this count. The city today stands next to the A1, the major road connecting the south to the north of England, and benefits from good railway links as well. The A1, running from London to Edinburgh is the latest in a long line of north–south routes: in the Middle Ages there was a road that ran along the Fen edge, and the

Romans had used nearby Ermine Street to send troops and provisions from London to York. The Fen Causeway was also an important east–west thoroughfare for them, and it is likely that it was already an important route in the Iron Age. In earlier times, the River Nene, too, had provided links to the Fens, other parts of England and, of course, sea ports; it was never a particularly deep river, but was easily able to accommodate the small cargo boats and lighters of earlier times.

The Romans certainly recognized Peterborough's strategic importance and built several garrisons around the area. It is possible that Durobrivae, a small walled town a few miles west of Peterborough, was the central administration point for all of the Fens. Although there are no written records, it is believed that the Fens formed an imperial estate of almost 1,100 square miles (300,000 hectares). The area provided much of the food for Roman troops garrisoned around East Anglia, and was referred to as the Roman Granary.

Once the Romans abandoned Britain to fend for itself, the Anglo-Saxons took over. During this period the area, which became known as Medehamstede, continued to serve as a distribution centre for Fen produce. The coming of the Church inaugurated a further rise in fortune. The early monastery there was founded by Peada, King of Middle Anglia, in 655. The legend is that Peada, who was the son of the pagan Penda, King of Mercia, wanted to marry a princess of the Northumbrian royal house. As her family were devout Christians, the union was only agreed to on the condition that Peada convert to Christianity. This he did, and to prove his newfound belief he caused the monastery to be built, appointing Saxulf as the first abbot. The monastery prospered and grew over the next couple of centuries but later, in common with other monastic houses in the area, it suffered at the hands of invading Vikings. There were several raids, but in 870 the abbey was completely sacked, and it was to be another hundred years before it regained its former glory. Although the Danish invaders did a lot of damage, many eventually settled peacefully here, as in other parts of East Anglia, and their influence is still evident today. Many Peterborough street names end in 'gate' (Queensgate, Priestgate, etc.), which comes from the Danish word *gata*, meaning street.

A wall was built around the monastery in around 1000, and at this time the town began to be known as Peterburh or Peterburch ('burch' being a form of *burgh*, 'fortified place', and 'Peter' stemming from the dedication of the abbey to St Peter). From 1052 to 1066, the abbey was fortunate to have been headed by a very shrewd abbot: Leofric, the nephew of Earl Leofric of Coventry and Lady Godiva. As well as undertaking building and improvements to the abbey, he increased the house's assets considerably – the abbey gained the alternative name of 'Gildenburch', or 'golden burgh', in reference to its wealth. Leofric was allied to King Harold, and so was deposed after the Norman triumph in 1066. Then, in 1070, the abbey suffered at the hands of an unexpected enemy. Hereward the Wake formed an unlikely alliance with the Danes to attack and loot the abbey, so as to keep its wealth out of the hands of William the Conqueror. As a result, the monastery was burnt to the ground, although the church survived – and William got it all in the end, anyway.

In 1116 the church was destroyed by fire and rebuilt much as it is today. The major change after that was political rather than structural. In 1539, the Dissolution of the Monasteries meant the administrative end of the abbey, but in 1541 the abbey church re-emerged as a cathedral. As was often the case, the abbot also re-emerged as the new bishop of the diocese.

All the while, the successful market town that had developed in the area surrounding the abbey grew and prospered. Like so many other English towns, it was devastated by the Black Death in the fourteenth century, but it recovered and was thriving again by Elizabethan times. Commerce was becoming increasingly organized and regulated. Interestingly, trading standards were in place even then: traders were prosecuted for selling food deemed 'detrimental to the health of the community', including 'missled pork' and 'naughty beef'.

In the sixteenth century two queens made their way to Peterborough, although neither was alive to enjoy the experience. In 1536, Catharine of Aragon, first wife of Henry VIII, died at Kimbolton in nearby Huntingdonshire and was buried at Peterborough Cathedral. From 1587 Mary Queen of Scots, executed at nearby Fotheringhay Castle, became a co-internee until her son, James I, had her remains removed to Westminster Abbey twenty-five years later. Shortly after that, the Civil War resulted in a great deal of damage, particularly to the Cathedral. The magnificent cloister windows, depicting various stories from the Old and New Testaments, the Kings of England and the foundation of the monastery were destroyed.

By Georgian times, the town still prospered as the smallest English cathedral city. In 1790 the population was some 3,000, but this was to increase dramatically in the next hundred years. In the early years of the nineteenth century a camp for French prisoners-of-war was established at nearby Norman Cross, and its population of prisoners outnumbered Peterborough's (there were 10,000 prisoners) when the camp closed in 1816. By 1851, the city's population was 8,763, and it increased to 17,429 over the next twenty years. This boom reflects the arrival of the railway in 1852; the Great Northern line from London to Scotland went through Peterborough and contributed greatly to its economic growth. For example, in 1861 some 2,000 of Peterborough's 11,732 inhabitants were employed by the railways – and others would have been engaged in occupations that serviced these workers, as well as businessmen and visitors. Businesses that depended on the railways to distribute their goods sprang up all over the place. One of the most significant was the large brickworks that opened in the late 1800s. Nowadays, Peterborough is very much a twenty-first-century city. It was designated a New Town in 1967 and has expanded considerably.

Smaller Market Towns

Many of the small towns in and around the Fens started off as market towns, which were often the only outlet for trade. People came from a surprisingly large surrounding area to sell their goods and buy things they could not themselves produce. (In Elizabethan times, a market town commonly served an area of about 100 square miles.)

Godmanchester

Just outside the Fens, Godmanchester was an important Roman fortress, which developed into a Roman town. Like Huntingdon, on the other side of the Great Ouse, it benefited from river traffic. A seventeenth century reference calls it 'a very great Toune', and it remained an important centre until the nineteenth century. Then common with so many other similar trade centres, Godmanchester declined as the railway took away the bulk of the river traffic. Today, it is a small, pleasant town lying in the shadow of the larger Huntingdon just across the river.

Huntingdon

Another town on the edge of the Fens, Huntingdon has known mixed fortunes over the centuries. Relics from the Palaeolithic and Neolithic eras have been uncovered in the area, and, because of the strategic position on the Great Ouse, it is likely that there has been a settlement of some sort there ever since. The town is first mentioned by that name c. 650, when it was known as 'Huntendune-porte' ('Huntendune' or Huntandun' means 'Hunter's Hill', and the suffix 'Porte' indicates that it was an important economic centre).

Huntingdon had its own mint, where coins were produced for local use between 855 and 1100, and it became a shire town in 921. The Domesday Survey of 1086 indicates a population of around 2000 – a thriving community – and like Norwich, Wisbech and Cambridge, it had a Norman castle, but this was demolished in 1174 and no buildings remain.

In 1205 King John incorporated Huntingdon as a town, and by the end of the thirteenth century, it was a major centre of population, with 16 parish churches within its boundaries. However, the Black Death hit the town badly, and by 1509 half the dwellings were empty. In 1599 Oliver Cromwell was born there and underwent some of his early education in the school at which Samuel Pepys was later a pupil. During the Civil War Cromwell had headquarters in Huntingdon for a time, and as a result the town was severely damaged by Royalists in 1645.

Later the town benefited from the growing coaching trade, which proved a valuable source of income for more than a century until the coming of the railway in 1850. In the twentieth century Huntingdon was one of the destinations for the London overspill scheme of the 1950s and 1960s, resulting in a significant increase in its population. With more than 19,000 inhabitants in 2002 it has proved popular with light industry and has three thriving industrial parks. Perhaps the most prominent resident of recent times has been John Major, Prime Minister of Britain from 1990 to 1997 and MP for Huntingdon for 22 years.

March

March is the administrative centre for the Fenland district. It is a town with a long railway tradition and is a centre for the distribu-

The immense damage that flood can cause

The flooded river breaks through the bank at Southery. This is just one of many
such breaches

All that is left of one family's possessions after the flood

Members of the Great Ouse Catchment Board planning and supervising the work of drainage and flood control

Diamond Jubilee celebrations in Littleport

The triangular bridge at Crowland. Today, cars and pedestrians pass under the bridge as the river has taken another route

The lock gates at Earith, now modernized

Lighters transporting cargo along the Old Bedford River in the nineteenth century

The enormous task of cleaning up after the flood gets under way

Pumping the floodwaters off the fields and into the rivers

Floodwaters break through the barrier bank

Breach in banks of River Wissey, letting the floodwaters on to fields and homes

tion of Fen produce. Today it has a population of over 18,000, benefiting from the good rail links. The March Trading Park has a range of sites of between one and fifteen acres, encouraging the diversification that is essential to the future of the Fens.

Ramsey

Ramsey Abbey was one of the five great Fenland abbeys in medieval times, and had tremendous power and influence (William Stukeley's *Itinerarium Curiosum* of 1724 refers to 'Ramsey Abbey, famous for its wealth, where every monk lived like a gentleman'). The abbey was founded in 971 by St Oswald, Bishop of Worcester. After the Dissolution of the Monasteries, its lands were given to Richard Williams, a nephew of Thomas Cromwell, Henry VIII's Chancellor of the Exchequer, who encouraged and supported him in his fight against the Vatican.

The suffix 'ey' or 'ea' denotes an island, or area that is higher than the surrounding marshes. It is believed that the name Ramsey means, quite simply, 'Ram's Island', in recognition of the sheep that would have grazed there, although 'island of wild garlic' (also known as ramsons) is another possible definition. Today Ramsey is a picturesque, if sleepy, little town in the heart of the Fens. Most industry there is based on agriculture and related trades.

St Ives

This Fen-edge town derived its prosperity from its location on the Great Ouse with easy access to surrounding Fenland. In about 1110 the abbot of Ramsey founded a fair here which soon became one of the most important trade markets in Europe, with merchants coming from Flanders, the Rhineland and northern France. Some of the most desirable goods sold there were fine cloths, and Henry III bought material at the fair for his royal robes. By the fourteenth century the fair was no longer of international importance, but it still did a good domestic trade.

The name St Ives derives from the legend of St Ivo, a bishop from Persia who is believed to have come to England, lived as a hermit and been buried in the village then called Slepe. When Ramsey Abbey was given the lordship of Slepe, a skull was discovered which the Abbot decided must be that of St Ivo. Although the skull was taken to the abbey, a small priory was built over the site of the grave at Slepe, and by about 1100 the town was starting to be known as St Ives.

Probably the most important historical site in St Ives is the famous chapel dedicated to St Leger, on the bridge. Visitors would pray there and leave money for the upkeep of the bridge. The bridge was built in 1415–26 on the site of an earlier wooden one; its four arches were destroyed as a defensive measure during he Civil War, but two were later rebuilt. After the Reformation, the chapel was put to various uses, including a public house. It eventually became derelict but was restored in 1929, though unfortunately the upper storeys had been demolished. The chapel is one of only three built on a bridge that survive in England today.

St Ives suffered much the same fate as Huntingdon, further upriver, when the railway arrived. However, it continues today as a market town, as well as home to some of the light industry spilling out of Silicon Fen.

Thorney

Another one of the great abbey towns, Thorney was first settled by monks c. 670. The monastery that grew up there was soon sacked by the Vikings but refounded in 972. It continued to prosper until the Dissolution of the Monasteries, when lands and assets were given to the Earl of Bedford. The original abbey church fell into ruin but was repaired in 1638 and exists today as the parish church of St Mary and St Botolph.

Many of today's residents are the descendants of refugees from France who laboured on the draining of the Fens and later settled in the town.

Wisbech

The town is known to some as 'The Capital of the Fens', and its story is closely aligned to the changing fortunes of the Fens. Until the mid-thirteenth century, the Rivers Ouse and Nene flowed to the sea at Wisbech. Then, probably due to excessive silting at the outfall, the rivers diverted to King's Lynn. This had a terrific impact on trade in Wisbech, which for a while had no inland navigation, but eventually the Nene returned to the town, and commerce was able to continue. By the fifteenth century, however, siltation was reaching a dangerous level again, and it was then that Bishop Morton made a new course for the Nene, Morton's Leam, to improve the situation.

Stone bridge at Wisbech

Once the Great Drainage of the seventeenth century was complete, Wisbech entered a time of prosperity. The nearby land was extremely fertile, and by the early nineteenth century the port was busy exporting corn and importing coal, timber and other goods.

The advent of the railways inevitably affected trade, but the port survived, perhaps because Wisbech Station was only on a small branch line. Today business in Wisbech, like so many other Fen market towns, is mainly related to the agricultural Fens. Indeed, much of Fenland's industry is located here, with 20 companies in the historic port area as well as 70 more on the industrial estate south-west of the town. There are producers of pet foods, poultry, canned food and apples. In addition there are engineering companies who build or customize lorry bodies.

Despite now being fourteen miles inland, each year the port services 100 ships, carrying up to 100,000 tonnes between them; vessels of up to 1,500 tonnes can be accommodated. Regular cargoes include timber and steel from Scandinavia and northern Europe and fertilizer, grain and animal feed from Holland. Plans for the future include increasing the leisure industry, and 150 metres of additional pleasure boat mooring are currently being developed.

12. Fen Agriculture Through the Ages

East Anglia, which includes the Fens, has more Grade I and Grade II agricultural land than anywhere else in Britain. (Grade I land is defined as having minor or no limitations for agricultural use; Grade II, only slightly less valuable, being identified as having only minor limitations.) Most of the peat lands in the Fens are designated Grade I, and most of the silt lands are Grade II. All sorts of crops are grown. The basis is a rotation of potatoes, wheat and sugar beet but, in addition, other cereal crops are grown, and so are vegetables (such as peas, beans, brassicas, carrots and celery) and fruit (such as strawberries). The Fens are also famous for the production of bulbs, as we shall see.

As well as good land, there is a favourable climate. Although there is a saying that 'The Fens have no climate, only a succession of weather', there is a pattern and it suits agriculture. Prevailing winds are mainly from the south and west, with colder north or north-easterly winds generally only in the early spring. Winds do play an important role in the Fen agricultural year, with Fen blows occurring on average three times a year; the fields are generally very open, and often windbreaks are employed to protect horticultural crops. Ironically, for a land once known as drowned, the area from Cambridge to the Wash is now the driest in Britain, with a mean annual rainfall of around 22 inches (560mm). Obviously, good irrigation is very important.

But how did this present situation come about? The changes over the years have been significant. The Romans seem to have been the first to farm the Fens intensively, draining portions of the land and growing barley to feed their troops. When they left, however, the Fens soon reverted to wet and unmanageable swamp in most places, and so there was not a great deal of agriculture during Anglo-Saxon times.

The higher ground could be cultivated or used to feed stock over the winter, but the rest was once again summer land, suitable only for coarse grazing and some hay-making during the drier months.

This pattern continued more or less unchanged for centuries. In the north of the area some farms grew corn and grass, and many shared common grazing land. The Norfolk and Lincoln breeds of sheep were grazed here – having no regard whatsoever for the wetness of the ground, they were ideal – and later became known throughout the country. Some Shire horses were also bred in the Fens and gained renown in the Midlands, which was the nearest main market for heavy horses.

It was, of course, the seventeenth century draining of the Fens that brought about big changes. The first crops grown on the peat Fens included hemp, flax, woad and mustard. A particularly favoured crop was cole-seed (now known as rape and still widely grown), which could be used both to feed sheep during the winter and to produce a saleable oil. The Fen sheep continued to be valued, and at the beginning of the eighteenth century their blood-lines were improved by crossing them with some Midland breeds. At around about the same time the potato was introduced and quickly became a major crop.

The agricultural revolution which began in the mid-to late eighteenth century, had an enormous effect all over Britain. A bigger population needed more food, farming methods became more intensive, and more and more grazing land was put to the plough. This is when the lives of people who lived on the Fens really began to change. No longer making their living from fishing and fowling and as shepherds, they became farm labourers and ploughmen. The area became very dependent on the fortunes of the farmers, and so suffered badly when the war with France ended in 1815. Wages fell, and the price of corn was halved. Shortly after that, labourers' wages were frozen at 9 shillings per week, and suddenly the cost of corn doubled in just one season. This led to riots all over the country, the worst of which on the Fens were the Littleport Riots of 1816.

Over the next few decades there were many improvements in farming methods. Mixed farming became the norm, with farmers specializing in a narrower range of products. New machinery made a huge difference. By the 1840s threshing machines were in common use, and soon after that, the McCormick reaper was imported from the United States. In 1890 there were reported to be

166

one million horses working in the Isle of Ely alone, but such was the impact of mechanization that by 1930 the number had dropped to 250,000, while crop yields had almost doubled.

Industry on the Fens was firmly based on agriculture, with companies springing up to manufacture farm machinery and other support products. Well-known manufacturers from this period include Richard Hornsby, Tuxford & Sons, and Clayton & Shuttleworth. A particularly successful manufacturer from King's Lynn, Frederick Savage, designed and developed equipment and then diversified; he became well-known for producing fairground equipment such as 'gallopers', 'razzle dazzles' and 'gondola switchbacks'.

The agricultural depression of the late nineteenth century inevitably caused hardship on the Fens, although the area suffered less than most. Unlike farmers in many others parts of the country, those on the Fens were not dependent on the profits from corn and beef. They were able to grow many other crops, such as vegetables and fruit; turnips, carrots and celery were among these crops that commanded good prices and grew well in the Fen soil. Sugar beet was introduced in the 1920s and proved a major success, as it is well suited to Fen soils and farming methods. In 1924 there were three sugar beet factories in the area, and by 1930 the acreage devoted to sugar beet production was doubling each year. By the 1970s almost all the sugar beet produced on the Fens was grown under contract to the British Sugar Corporation, which owned sugar beet factories at Ely, Peterborough, Spalding, Wissington and King's Lynn.

By the middle of the twentieth century, potatoes were a major Fen product, with 36% of the UK main crop originating there. Potato farming is a science in itself, as this is not an easy crop to grow, being subject to potato blight, aphids and potato cyst eelworm. Nevertheless, the Fen farmers made a success of the market, producing enough potatoes during the growing season to enable thousands of tons to be stored and then sold as late as the spring of the following year. Storage was initially in straw clamps, but controlled-environment storage buildings were developed and used increasingly.

By the mid-1970s the change from mixed agriculture based on a combination of livestock and arable, to solely arable farming, was largely complete. By then only 10% of farm income derived from livestock or livestock products. Cereals accounted for a greater acreage than any other crop – partly on account of a problem unique to the Fens: as the peat shrank, it became less and less suitable for root crops.

By the middle of the 1970s some 100,000 acres of Fen had no peat cover left, and had become mixtures of sand or clay and silt. Although these fields were no longer so fertile, farmers became very progressive, coming up with means to make use of the peatless land. As the peat continues to drop at the rate of approximately one inch each year, such innovation is of increasing importance.

Where the ground still has a good peat cover, it remains fertile and comparatively easy to work. However, there is another problem with the peat soil – it is not just cash crops that grow well in it. Weeds flourish in the rich ground; consequently the development and use of pesticides and other pest control measures has become a key factor in prosperity.

Today there is little left of the old livestock tradition in the Fens. One or two dairy herds do still remain, though, and the washlands are still used, as they have been for centuries, for summer grazing. It is mainly cattle and sheep that are seen in the fields and on the banks of the river, although the Black Fens (peat Fens) are best known for producing pigs.

Horticulture

Missing from the above account is the story of horticulture on the Fens. This is largely a fairly modern development, being dependent on the quick distribution of produce or on preserving processes such as freezing and canning. Horticulture, in its original sense of the art of gardening, goes back to at least Roman times, when apple orchards were introduced. In the sixteenth and seventeenth centuries Flemish immigrants grew onions and sold them at the Peterborough and Stourbridge fairs, and there was a large fruit-producing area around Wisbech, again mainly supplying local towns.

However, large-scale horticulture really came to the fore with the advent of the railways, which facilitated transport of the produce to distant urban centres. The impact of railways can be seen in the example of Stephen Chivers and his son John who in 1850 were growing fruit on three acres (1.2 ha) of land at Histon, just outside Cambridge, for supply to local markets. By 1860 they had 160 acres

(65 ha), and by the end of the 1800s this had increased to 3,000 acres (1,214 ha); in 1873 they opened a jam factory, and in 1894 were the first to preserve fruit in cans.

Fruit crops included apples, plums, strawberries and other soft fruit. Tomatoes were grown, and in 1894 Gautry & Thoday had two acres of outdoor tomatoes as well as some being grown under glass. Exotic vegetables also proved to be in demand, and specialities such as asparagus were very profitable. By 1891 fruit was being grown on 2,000 acres (809 ha) in Cambridgeshire and the Isle of Ely and 1,300 acres (526 ha) in Holland in Lincolnshire. This increased to 3,500 and 1,700 acres (1,416 and 688 ha) respectively at the peak. In the early 1900s flowers became a very popular crop, and acres around Willingham, Rampton and Cottenham, north of Cambridge, were given over to such blooms as pyrethrums and chrysanthemums.

The area around Wisbech became a major horticultural centre, and Kentish immigrants settled there at the end of the nineteenth century and expanded the tradition. The first orchards were owned by H.H. Bath and J. Cockett. Bath, the larger of the two producers, was growing vegetables and fruit on over 600 acres (240 ha) of land by 1890 and employing more than 1,000 pickers during the strawberry season. They also produced flowers, packing and shipping over 100,000 pansies and violets a day.

By the second half of the twentieth century, horticulture was continuing to do well, supplying urban centres with fruit and vegetables, as well as supplying the canners and jam-makers. Chatteris became the carrot centre of Britain, and three-quarters of Britain's celery crop was grown around Ely, Littleport and Southery. Each year millions of celery seedlings were raised under glass around Whittlesey before being planted out on the peat fields, where the soil is perfect for the crop. Onions became a significant Fen product, with farmers successfully attempting to compete with Spanish imports.

Which leads on to bulbs. Although most people today would identify the Fens as a major bulb-growing area, this is a relatively recent phenomenon. In 1885 hardly any bulbs were grown commercially; a directory for Spalding – now a major bulb-growing area – listed only one producer (a Mrs Quincey, who specialized in snowdrops and narcissi), but by 1892 seventy-five growers were listed. The sudden popularity of bulbs was the result, at least in part, of the emergence of the middle classes who, having some spare time and cash, became interested in domestic gardening. Perhaps the first to tap into this market was a company called J. and H. Gostelow, which started out by sending narcissus bulbs in an old hat box to Covent Garden. Another early producer was Richard Wellband, who was one of the first to force daffodils under glass.

Tulips are perhaps associated with the Fens more than any other bulb flower. In addition to those sold around the country, millions of tulips are produced each year for the Spalding bulb festival, which remains an international event. As well as tulips and the other bulbs mentioned above, the area produces gladioli, iris, peonies and freesias. Spalding is also the centre of a glasshouse industry producing plants for the home.

By the middle of the twentieth century, the acreage devoted to bulbs had tripled, accounting for more than 30% of Fenland farm output, and the area had become the biggest horticultural market in England. Today a far more significant area is given over to cereals and vegetables, but the bulb industry nonetheless remains a very real part of the agricultural identity of the Fens.

13. Fenland Nature and Supernature

The Fens have always abounded with wildlife. Generations of Fenmen survived by exploiting the fish and eels in the rivers, as well as the various types of wild birds that thrived in the marsh grasses and muddy swamps. They also cut reeds and used them for all sorts of purposes, from building and thatching to making baskets for catching eels and nets for catching birds. And the ever-present peat was an invaluable source of fuel for cooking and heating.

The Fenmen's greatest fear about drainage was that it would change all this, as the land dried out and the wildlife habitats and vegetation disappeared. They were at least partially justified in that fear, for the land certainly has changed. What had been a larder full of fish and wildfowl became the breadbasket of Britain, with field upon field of grain, potatoes and multitudinous other crops. And yet the Fens remained an attractive area for wildfowl, and even now there are plenty of fish to be found. Keen fishermen come from all over to take advantage of the excellent fishing in Fen rivers, and wildfowl still abounds and acts as a draw for sportsmen.

But the draining of the Fens and, in particular, the creation of the Washes has added a whole new element to wildlife on the Fens. Ironically, in making an artificial environment Man has unintentionally created a haven for all sorts of birds, animals, insects, fish and plants – not just the fish and fowl that have always lived on the Fens, but also newcomers attracted by the man-made landscape.

The Ouse Washes, an integral part of the Fens, is the largest area of regularly flooded washland in Britain, making it a winter haven for migratory (and non-migratory) wildfowl. Also the intermittently flooded areas are of little agricultural use, which makes them very attractive to water birds, as they provide food, nesting sites and protection from predators. Moreover, the chemical fertilizers and pesticides prevalent in so many other parts of Britain are not present to such a great degree (some inevitably find their way into the Washes via the river system, but the chemical mix is a great deal less deadly here than in many other places). All in all, it is not hard to see why birds come from all over the world. Once again, the Fens are playing their role as a land out of time; if many of the sites that once were suitable for the birds are now intensively farmed agricultural land, disturbed by constant cultivation and spraying, the Washes remain friendly. And so, too, do the coastal areas around the Wash, which are highly attractive to sea birds, wildfowl and waders. The salt marshes and tidal flats, extending for miles along the coast, create a very special environment that draws many different varieties of wildlife in large numbers.

All sorts of birds, plants and invertebrates make their home on the Fens. Other residents who have been here for centuries but nonetheless benefit from the current environment, include owls, bats and butterflies. Many of these species are threatened with extinction, and yet manage to survive in the Fens.

Birds

Some birds live on the Fens all year long, whilst others are migratory visitors from abroad. The Washes are particularly noted for the communities of ruff, a wading bird with spectacular breeding plumage. The black-tailed godwit, with its long slender legs, emulates the old Fen Slodgers on their stilts and is eminently suited to a Fen existence. Many other species of wader also live and breed on the Washes.

They are joined by nationally rare breeding species such as the quail and the spotted crake and a small breed of falcon called the hobby. The brilliant blue-green kingfisher is another bird ideally suited to the Washes, as it feeds on fish and aquatic insects; it uses the bones from the fish to line the nest that it tunnels into the river bank.

There are many more. The heron is another bird that can negotiate the Fens on its own in-built stilts. There are ducks aplenty – teal, wigeon, gadwall, pintail, pochard, mallard and tufted – as well as the shoveler, which uses its long, broad, flattened beak to filter-feed in the surface water. Also present are the moorhen and the great crested grebe, with its brightly coloured head crest and cheek tippets.

172

The most impressive visitors must be the swans who make their way to the Washes every winter. Some 4,000 Bewick's swans arrive from Arctic Siberia, and are joined by 1,500 whooper swans from Iceland. The whooper, a magnificent bird, weighs about 24 pounds (more or less the weight of a terrier), while the Bewick's is a little smaller, at around 11 to 17 pounds. Both species mate for life, and many begin their courtships on the Washes, where they overwinter at the Wildfowl and Wetland Trust at Welney. The WWT knows when to expect its guests and arranges special evenings when spectators can watch the incredible sight of thousands of these beautiful birds coming in to feed.

Plants and Invertebrates

Less spectacular perhaps, but equally important, are the plants and invertebrates of the Fens. Marsh and damp grasslands predominate on the Washes, where more than 300 species of higher plants flourish. These include ribbon-leaved plantain and least lettuce, both rare and protected species. Nationally scarce species including the Fringed Yellow Water-lily and River Water Dropwort do well in the Old Bedford River and the River Delph. In various parts of the Washes can be seen stunning displays of Purple Loosestrife, Great Willowherb and Marsh Woundwort, looking as wonderful as their names sound. And for those who like mucking about in the mud, an extremely rich variety of invertebrates can be found in the ditches, rivers and ponds of the Washes.

Conservation and Its Problems

The Fens have attracted a good deal of attention from national and international conservation bodies. As a haven for a number of different species of birds, plants and invertebrates, large parts of the area have been designated a Site of Special Scientific Interest (SSSI). It is also a Special Protection Area (SPA) for birds and, under the 1971 Ramsar Convention, is acknowledged as an internationally important wetland area.

The Wildfowl and Wetland Trust Centre at Welney is one place that maintains a healthy habitat for wild birds and encourages them to nest and breed on the Washes. There is also the Wicken Fen

National Nature Reserve, operated by the National Trust. Wicken Fen is the country's oldest nature reserve and is dedicated to recreating the Fens as they were before drainage. All sorts of flora and fauna thrive there as they would nowhere else today.

Various other conservation interests have a strong presence on the Washes. The Royal Society for the Protection of Birds has a reserve on the Washes near Welches Dam. Other societies involved with the Fens include English Nature, The Wildlife Trust for Bedfordshire, Cambridgeshire, Northamptonshire and Peterborough, and the Norfolk, Suffolk and Lincolnshire Wildlife Trusts. And, of course, as the government body charged with protecting the environment, the Environment Agency plays a very big role.

This, however, can lead to conflict. As we have seen, much of the wildlife living on the Fens today has been attracted by the creation of the Washes. But it has to be remembered that the Washes and all the other flood-defence devices on the Fens, such as rivers and sluices and pumps, were designed solely for the purpose of draining the land and keeping it drained. That a wildlife-friendly habitat also results is purely a happy coincidence.

It takes a lot of continuous work and maintenance to keep the Washes working properly as a flood defence mechanism, and, unfortunately, some of that work does not make the conservation bodies happy. For example, it is vital that the rivers and drains be kept clear of silt and vegetation, so that they can flow freely; failing to do this would simply result in floods. So, each year, work is carried out to make sure that the rivers run freely. That involves scouring where necessary to remove excess silt, and also regularly cutting back vegetation in and along the rivers. Left to themselves, the reeds and riverside grasses would soon grow out into the rivers and obstruct them – and rivers that don't have a healthy flow become increasingly clogged up, which in turn creates flooding.

The basis of the problem is that work to maintain the Washes can also threaten the wildlife that has decided it's such a nice place to live in. Those responsible for flood defence and land drainage would like to clear the rivers of unwanted vegetation at least twice a year – in late spring and autumn – cutting back the reeds, etc., when they are at their worst. However, in the spring the birds are nesting in those reeds and grasses, and if the rivers were 'mowed' at the ideal time for flood defence, thousands of nests would be destroyed and countless nestlings killed. Understandably, the conservation interests campaign vigorously for the mowing to take place at a more bird-friendly time of year.

Here is where things get even stickier. Since 1996 the Environment Agency has been charged with responsibility for various aspects of the environment. To quote its website: 'The Agency has an important role in conservation and ecology. We can help create an environment where wildlife can thrive, especially along rivers and in wetlands. We help achieve [the aims of the UK Biodiversity Plan] by protecting and enhancing wildlife'. However, the Agency has also been given the job of Flood Defence. And although it takes its role as 'Guardian of the Environment' very seriously, there is no getting around the fact that flood defence is a very major part of its remit; in fact, that accounts for the great majority of its budget. That about £200 million is spent in England on flood and coastal defences every year, is perhaps not surprising, because failure to maintain flood defences would swiftly result in loss of land, property and, quite likely lives.

This is a circle that the Environment Agency tries very hard to square, and it participates in numerous studies, groups and plans designed to solve the problem. But there is still a bottom line: the vegetation cannot be allowed to dam up the rivers. In recent years a compromise has been reached and, in many places, the Agency cuts the rivers only once a year at a time when birds are not nesting. This practice does pose a potential risk to the free flow of the rivers, so essential to keeping the floods at bay, but as yet the compromise seems not to have caused great problems. Certainly this reduced maintenance cannot realistically be blamed for the floods of recent years. Nevertheless, it is worrying to take a trip down a Fenland river in the autumn and see just how much the reeds and grasses have encroached on the waterway. In places the reeds growing on either side almost meet in the middle, and there can be no doubt this must affect river flows. Like the shrinking peat, this is another flood-defence predicament that the drainage men manage to merely cope with, not solve – just one more aspect of Man's battle against Nature on the Fens.

The Supernatural

Alongside the natural flora and fauna, the Fens have more than their fair share of superstitions and supernatural strangeness – not surprising, given the nature of the land itself, which in its almost unremitting flatness and lack of dramatic features can be eerie. Perhaps it has something to do with the feeling of vulnerability that comes with such wide open spaces, or with the overwhelming, ever-present three-quarter sky.

One of the most common manifestations of evil was the will o' the wisp. This was a bright light which shone over the fields and marshes, seeming to move with a will of its own. And, indeed, it did move and it did exist. For the will-o'-the-wisp (also known as a jack-o'-lantern) is a natural phenomenon. Far more common in the days before drainage, this supposedly evil creature was simply a light created by the spontaneous combustion of marsh gases and blown about on the wind. Ancient Fenmen imagined that the light was alive and a creature of the Devil (though not everyone held it in such awe: another, more jocular name for the jittering light was Jinny Burntarse).

One thing that was universally feared, however, was the hound of hell known as Black Shuck. It is not known where the belief in an evil dog who walks the Fens came from, although it is likely to have originated with the Danes who invaded and eventually settled in the Fens. Black Shuck is the ghostly descendant of the black hound that belonged to the fearsome Scandinavian god, Odin. Seeing this canine spectre stalking through the trees was meant to portend certain and terrifying death. Similarly, sighting the ghosts of dead men rising out of the marshes was a dreadful omen of death and disaster. Either or both of these spectres may have been further manifestations of the marsh gas.

Other Fen superstitions, although not without their dark or bizarre side, involved protective charms. These included wearing dried eel-skin 'garters' to ward off rheumatism, or rubbing a wart away with a raw potato. Allegedly, pregnancy could be averted by drinking vinegar in which pennies from the church collection had been soaked; if that failed, the second option was rather more odious, as it involved holding hands with a corpse. Placing a roasted onion in the ear was said to banish earache, and eating a roast mouse would cure both whooping cough and smallpox.

Witches

Witches were a common feature of Fen life. Often women (or men) who had a special knack with animals or understood the properties of certain herbs and plants, they were an accepted part of Fen life for centuries. No doubt they had always been held in awe and varying degrees of fear, but witches did not really face persecution until the infamous witch trials began in the sixteenth century.

Perhaps the best-known and best-documented persecution of a so-called witch took place just on the edge of the Fens in Warboys in the late 1500s. It is more than likely that the whole unpleasant episode was caused by malicious children. In 1589 the Throckmorton household consisted of Robert Throckmorton and his wife, four daughters, two sons, a grandmother and several servants; by all accounts, the children were unruly, particularly the girls. Living next to them were John and Alice Samuels (or Samwells) and their daughter, Agnes. It is believed that the Samuels disapproved of the indiscipline next door, and Alice, at least, was heard to say that she would not allow a child of hers to carry on as the Throckmortons did.

Young Jane Throckmorton, then ten years old, suddenly began having fits of a very odd nature, involving prolonged sneezing and convulsions and faints. A doctor was called, but he could not establish their cause. Within a month all the girls were afflicted, and still no medical reason could be found. One doctor asked if the family thought witchcraft could be a factor, and Mr Throckmorton said he did not. His daughter Jane, though, obviously had other ideas. One day she pointed out their neighbour, Alice Samuels, to her grandmother, saying 'Grandmother, look where the old witch sitteth. Did you ever see one more like a witch than she is ... I cannot abide to look upon her.'

The whole episode lasted for about a year and went through a series of bizarre permutations. For a time, Alice Samuels was actually employed to live in the Throckmorton house and look after the girls, as it was only in her presence that the fits subsided. At one point all the servants came down with the same inexplicable malady and left – only to find that their symptoms disappeared once they left the house – and, allegedly, their replacements came down with the same malady. Lady Cromwell, Oliver Cromwell's aunt, visited the family, accused Alice of witchcraft and died herself some fifteen months later.

The coincidences (and, most likely, the conspiracy) escalated until eventually Alice, her husband and young daughter were carted off to be tried. The usual threats and torture soon sent Alice (who was probably already near the end of her tether) completely insane, and she confessed to being a witch, in the employ of the Devil and everything else the torturers asked for. The whole family, including the daughter, were hanged at Huntingdon in 1593.

Throughout the Fens there is evidence in the belief in witches. People would make up witch bottles. Fashioned in clay and often containing nail or hair clippings, these were designed to look like the witch in question (or perhaps simply the enemy in question) and stuck through with needles. They were hidden in rafters and ceilings or simply buried; hundreds have been found in old houses and barns on the Fens. Rather similar to these were 'hexes' of solid mud or clay, moulded to resemble an enemy and buried or hidden.

14. The Fens Today and Tomorrow

Today

At the beginning of the twenty-first century, the Fens continue to be a major food-producing area, contributing significantly to the output from East Anglia as a whole. A quarter of all the cereals grown in England comes from East Anglia, as well as almost a third of the potatoes. Approximately 50,000 people are employed in farming, and another 50,000 in related industries, which include processing, packaging, agricultural engineering and haulage. Over half the land on the Fens is devoted to growing cereals or root crops, and the Wisbech area is still renowned for its orchards, producing apples and berries of all sorts. Horticulture, too, remains an important part of the picture, with the Fens producing peas, beans, berries, bulbs and flowers for the rest of the nation. And sugar beet retains its importance – more than half England's crop is grown in the Fens.

Although livestock became relatively less important after drainage, it is still an important industry. The area has England's second-largest pig herd, numbering 1.4 million animals. Poultry production is also big business, with more than two million eggs laid every day and 19 million chickens produced for food annually.

Farmers across Britain have had a hard time in recent years, and those on the Fens are no exception. Fen farms vary in size from just a few to several thousand acres, but the trend towards amalgamation into fewer and larger farms continues. This may help yields and profits but it presents a problem for those who traditionally made their living working the farms: larger farms and ever-increasing mechanization reduce the numbers of men required to work each acre of land. And Britain's entry in the Common Market has

179

brought its own set of headaches for the farming industry; rulings from Brussels can and do result in reduced farm incomes, despite better yields. As always, Fen farmers have responded to this challenge with enterprise and innovation. There is increasing diversification into unusual crops, opening up and exploring new markets. Many farms have negotiated business links with the large multiple retailers and sell direct (in some cases, exclusively), to the giant supermarket chains.

Industry on the Fens remains closely linked to food production, although there is a growing emphasis on other industry. A quick look at the major employers in Fenland shows that well over half are involved in food processing and/or packaging. However, there are also analysts, safety clothing manufacturers, brick-makers and precision engineers, so diversification is increasing all the time. It is hoped that more and more of the high-tech industries currently located in and around Cambridge will move or expand northwards into the Fens.

As always, the successors of the Breedlings and Fen Tigers meet challenges and threats to survival with courage and determination. It is telling to note that one in every six workers in the Fens today is self-employed.

Tomorrow

The future can never be predicted. Certainly events of the past shape the future, and this is perhaps more true on the Fens than in many other places. Man changed the land to suit his own purpose, and that endeavour, whilst creating a rich and fertile agricultural land, had its drawbacks. Mistakes were made that remain with us today.

The shrinkage of the Fens, which was caused by draining the peat lands, is a major problem – and one to which there appears to be no solution. Already some farmers have come to the end of the line, in that their ploughs are now hitting the hard, buttery clay underneath the peat: not much will grow in that. But still the Fens continue to shrink. What can be done to stop that? The question seems unanswerable.

Although government, farmers and everyone concerned are aware of the problem, there does seem to be an element of hoping that it will go away if ignored. (It won't, of course.) That is not to suggest that there are not many people involved in trying to find an answer. It is just that, although the enormity of the problem is acknowledged, there is no contingency plan for what to do when the inevitable occurs. And, barring a miracle or some incredible technical innovation, it must be inevitable: land that has been shrinking for four hundred years is not going to stop doing so suddenly of its own accord. And, as we have seen, there is a bottom line – the buttery clay. At least it's a bottom as far as agriculture is concerned.

There are other problems. The end of the 1990s saw the start of a new cycle of flooding, and although the mechanisms in place to limit flood damage are impressive, there were inevitable losses. It is very likely that such disasters will continue through the next decade and perhaps more. This is not just caused by the shrinking of the Fens, it is a world-wide problem caused by climatic change. According to the Environment Agency, changing climate patters in the UK mean we will be seeing ten percent more annual rainfall and wetter winters – bad news for everyone, but especially bad for the Fens.

In a recent interview with the BBC, Environment Agency Chairman John Harman detailed all that was being done to limit potential damage and advised that £300 million is spent each year on flood-defence. But he went on to warn that no amount of flood-defence work could guarantee against flood. As he said, 'You can't fight Nature all the time'.

But isn't that what the men of the Fens have been doing for centuries? Ever since the Breedlings lost their battle to keep their land as it was, Man has been fighting Nature. And perhaps that is the key. Perhaps the future will see Man return to working with Nature again. After all, although theirs was an incredibly harsh existence, that is what the Breedlings, the original Fen Tigers, did for so long: they learned to live, to survive, sometimes even to flourish in natural conditions.

Or maybe once again the Adventurers' spirit will prevail. Maybe Man will win through, using ingenious plans and innovative technology to override Nature's default setting. It has been done before on the Fens. We wait to see.

APPENDIXES

I. Technical Facts

The on-going attempts to make the Fens more habitable have led to some remarkable feats of engineering. The fact that the rivers and drains made centuries ago were largely dug out by hand does not detract from the engineering skills involved in their creation. For example, when the Old Bedford River was made as the first step in Vermuyden's plan for draining the Fens, thousands of men laboured for many months to remove tons of earth to form the river. They had no sophisticated equipment but used simple forks, picks, spades and barrows. Even when the river was dug, that was not the end of the task. Embankments had to be built up on the sides to keep the water contained therein. These were largely comprised of the earth that had been removed to create the drain in the first place, so there was an economy of materials, if not of labour.

The creation of the Ouse Washes as a flood storage reservoir in the seventeenth century was what really brought about the Fens as they are today. Very possibly it was the single most important event in the modern history of the Fens. Certainly it changed the land and the lives of those who lived on it.

As has already been shown, the Ouse Washes are a flood-defence mechanism – as much a machine as anything made up of cogs and wheels or electronic circuits and switches. The components of this machine are rivers and drains, sluices, embankments and pumps. The Washes have already been described in broad outline, so this section is for those who might wish to understand the machine in more detail.

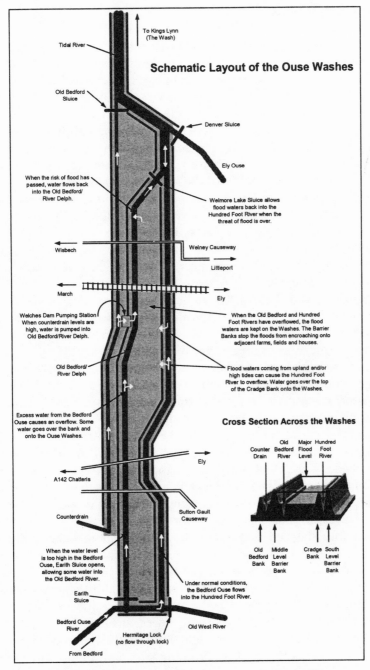

Schematic diagram of the Ouse Washes from Earith to Denver

Creating a Washland

A washland is defined as 'an area of land periodically flooded by overflow water from a river, stream or from the sea'. The Ouse Washes, which are the largest area of regularly flooded washland in Britain, have to perform two functions. First of all, they must be able to store flood waters effectively, keeping the excess water off adjoining farms, fields and properties, including 830 homes. Next, there must be efficient arrangements for conveying the waters back into the rivers and drains when the flood subsides, so that they can then be carried away safely to the sea. This is achieved by a system of sluices, pumps and embankments that runs for 20 miles (32 km) from Earith in the south to Denver in the north. The system is about 5/8 mile (1 km) across at its widest point. The aim is to protect towns and villages in this area as well as some 70,000 acres (28,000 ha) of valuable agricultural land. The diagram shows the integrated system and how it works.

It all starts at Earith where, when there is too much water flowing down the Bedford Ouse, the sluice opens to allow some of the water to be diverted into the Old Bedford River, which was the first major artificial river made by Vermuyden. Normally, the water would flow into the Hundred Foot River, Vermuyden's second major cut. Both rivers are embanked, forming a sort of corridor between them: that corridor is the Ouse Washes. When water is thus diverted into the Old Bedford River, levels inevitably begin to rise and some of its flows out of the Old Bedford and on to the Washes. Similarly, if the level in the Hundred Foot River on the other side of the Washes gets too high, some of that also overflows on to the Washes. The flood waters are stored between the Barrier Banks, which protect adjacent farms and other properties. When the danger of flood has passed, the water is allowed to flow back either into the Old Bedford or through Welmore Lake Sluice to rejoin the Hundred Foot River and then on to Denver and finally the sea. The path of the water can be seen in the diagram.

There are many parts to this mechanism, all of which must be maintained and improved to keep the Washes functioning effectively. In addition to the locks and sluices, an essential component, which became common in the eighteenth century, was the windmill, used to pump water off the shrinking land and up into the rivers. These 'engines' soon became a common sight on the Fens (there were over 2,000 of them before they were superseded by steam-driven pumps). Almost all were made in the Dutch fashion, with manually operated tailpoles rather than fantails. The largest, at Soham Mere, had a sail span of 80 feet (24m), paddles a foot (30cm) wide and a scoop wheel that was more than 18 feet (5.5m) in diameter. This windmill, built in 1867 and finally demolished in 1948, could drain 500–600 acres (200–240 ha) of land.

The steam pumps, which took over from the wind engines in the early 1800s, were so well built that most had a working life of over a hundred years. The first, a 12-hp engine, was installed in 1817 at Sutton St Edmund, and the first in the southern Fens, at Ten Mile Bank, arrived in 1819 (this one had two scoop wheels). The typical pump was a single-cylinder, double-acting, low-pressure beam engine. Like the windmills before them, these engines drove a scoop wheel. Their capacity was far greater, though, and the largest had an output of 80-hp and could drain 8,000–10,000 acres (3,200–4,000 ha) – about sixteen times as much as a windmill. They were magnificent and heavy pieces of machinery. (The scoop wheels alone, which had cast iron centres, were enormous. The heaviest was the one on the Hundred Foot Pump – which was 50 feet in diameter and weighed 75 tonnes.) The weight caused a special problem in the Fens because of the nature of the shrinking peat. Special foundations had to be built so that the pumping equipment didn't sink into the soil. Sometimes concrete and gravel were used, but the most common method was to drive hundreds of piles and cross timbers into the earth; blocks of masonry sat upon this structure, and the pump sat on top of the masonry.

After 1851 centrifugal pumps began to replace scoop wheels. Some steam engines were used until 1947, but they began to be replaced in 1913 by diesel driven machines – which were themselves superseded from 1948 onwards by automatic electric motors.

The twentieth century saw many other improvements and modifications, the most recent of which are detailed below.

Welmore Lake Sluice

The new sluice at Welmore is a very significant element in the fight against flooding. Its importance lies in the fact that the sluice at Welmore Lake is the only means of getting water off the Ouse

Washes and into the Hundred Foot River, which eventually takes it to the sea. At Welmore Lake in Norfolk, 20 kilometres south of King's Lynn, the River Delph* and the Tidal River (Ouse) meet. The first part of the task at Welmore is to hold back and store excess water during times of flood. Once the worst of the flood is over, this water is allowed to flow through and rejoin the Hundred Foot River and so reach the sea. But, in the process, the Sluice must also keep the salt water of the Tidal River out of the River Delph and the Ouse Washes.

At least two structures have stood at Welmore Lake since the first embankment was built there in 1756. The first sluice was built in 1825 and replaced by a more modern construction in 1933. However, by the end of the 1990s, this too was beginning to show its age, and in 1997 work began on an improved replacement. Perhaps the most obvious change was to relocate the sluice about 70 metres downstream, closer to where the River Delph meets the Hundred Foot River. This reduced the build up of silt, which is a major problem in the Ouse Washes, not least at Welmore. The fine particles quickly clog up the rivers, dangerously slowing the flow of water. The problem tends to be self-perpetuating, because silt accumulates when the rivers are running sluggishly; this further hinders the flow of water, which leads to more silt build up. Anything that encourages the rivers to flow vigorously is of great importance, so, whereas the old structure had only two sluiceways, the new one has three, increasing the amount of water that can flow through by 50%.

Other improvements include a permanent pumping facility and a purpose-built system of high-pressure silt-jetting nozzles designed to help prevent a build-up of silt around the sluice.

The reconstruction was an ambitious project with interesting technical details, including a temporary cofferdam (a watertight structure that is pumped dry to allow work on structures that are normally under water to take place in the dry). The new sluice was built within a 45-metre diameter cofferdam. A length of the south bank of the River Delph was excavated to divert water flow around

---

* Downstream (north) of Welches Dam the river is called the Delph and upstream (south) it is the Old Bedford or Forty Foot River. *Old* Bedford is the name given to Vermuyden's first effort which is, of course, 40 foot wide and *New* Bedford is (sometimes) attributed to his second effort which is 100 foot wide.

the cofferdam, so that the Washes could still function effectively while the work was going on. Interesting technical details include:

- The sluice has three upstream vertical steel lift gates, approximately 7.4 metres wide and 6.7 metres high, each weighing 25 tonnes.
- The three pairs of mitre gates are 4.7 metres x 7.0 metres. Each gate weighs 12 tonnes. They are made of ekki timber, a sturdy tropical hardwood from sustainable sources.
- The permanent pumping installation utilizes two submersible canister-type pumps installed in chambers in the upstream end of the piers.

Denver Sluice

There has been a sluice at Denver since the seventeenth century (except between 1713, when the sluice was destroyed by tides, and 1750, when a replacement was built). An improved structure took over in 1834. This was designed by the famous engineer, Sir John Rennie, and his three sluice gates still exist today, although improvements have been made and a lot of other components added over the years.

Today the site is referred to as the Denver Complex, reflecting the many different components that make up the whole. Two structures are in place primarily for flood defence. They are Denver Sluice itself, next to which stands the Navigation Lock, allowing boats to travel between Denver and the Middle Level (the area of Fenland north of the Hundred Foot Washes) and also down the Tidal River to the Wash. Further along is the A.G. Wright Sluice, sometimes referred to as the Head Sluice, which was a direct response to the dreadful floods of 1947. It was built between 1956 and 1958 and acts as the gateway to the Relief Channel. As its name implies, the Relief Channel was built to relieve the Tidal River of freshwater flood flows, particularly at times when the river's performance is compromised by the incoming tide. As well as providing a second conduit for floodwaters, it was also built sufficiently large to store, or buffer, floodwater until tides recede and allow discharge out through the tail sluice at King's Lynn.

Denver also has structures designed to deal with the problems of water supply. In the 1960s, the Government saw an impending water shortage in south Essex, due to expansion and population increase. It was decided to solve this problem by transferring surplus water from the Ely Ouse to the headwaters of the Essex rivers. Surplus water from the Ely Ouse area is transferred to the Cut-off channel at Denver. This is water that would eventually have drained to the sea – far better to send it where it is needed. At Denver the Impounding Sluice enables the water level in the channel to be raised by about 2 feet (0.6m), which produces a reversal of flow, and the water then travels backwards for 15 miles (25 km) to Blackdyke in Hockwold. From there it is drawn off into a tunnel 12 miles (20 km) long that ends up at Kennet. Still the journey isn't over. The water is pumped into a 9 mile (14 km) pipeline and ends up in the River Stour at Kirtling Green; some water is pumped even further to the River Pant. The water from Denver travels by a rather circuitous route: 88 miles (141 km) through pipelines to the Abberton reservoir and 92 miles (148 km) to the Hanningfield reservoir, both in Essex. But the system works, taking water from where there is often far too much of it to where it is needed – and for two-thirds of its journey the water travels along existing watercourses.

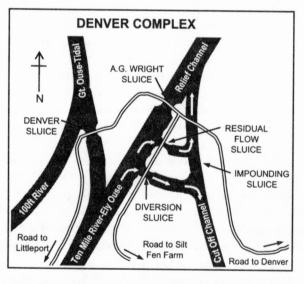

The Denver Complex, showing the position of the five sluices and diversion channel.

Other Recent Improvements

Work on the Ouse Washes system is continuous. Recent projects include improvements to the Barrier Banks and Welches Dam Pumping Station.

The Barrier Banks are, of course, a vital component of the system. Something has to keep the water in the flood storage reservoir, and the Barrier Banks take on a large part of this task. Without them, the Fens would flood all the way to Peterborough and Ely. More than 230 homes would be in danger if the South Level Barrier Bank failed. Up to 27,000 acres (11,000 ha) of arable land would be flooded, and there is a very real chance that lives would be lost. The potential damage of such a disaster is estimated at £23 million. But if the Middle Level Barrier Bank were to fail the toll would be even worse, with more than 600 homes and 44,500 acres (18,000 ha) of agricultural land flooded at a cost of some £42 million.

Just to give an idea of the work required of the Banks, major flooding in 1998 meant that the Banks held a massive 60 million cubic metres of water on the Washes, keeping it off adjacent farms and properties. Even more astonishingly, this water was held at a level five metres above the surrounding land.

The importance of maintaining the integrity of these Banks is obvious. Several factors combine to put them at risk. The first is the ongoing problem of the shrinking land. In some places, the level of the land in relation to the sea has fallen 16 feet (5m) since the Barrier Banks were first built back in the seventeenth century. Added to that is the fact that there has been a steady rise in sea levels over the years. Erosion is another problem. Recently £14 million was spent to raise and reprofile the Middle Level Barrier Bank, and another £6 million on strengthening the South Level Barrier Bank.

Embankments were very probably the first method used to control flooding, later supplemented by pumps. The earliest pumps were primarily intended to take water off the shrinking land up into the rivers, channels and drains. Indeed, that is usually the function of today's modern pumps. However, in the Middle Level, Welches Dam Pumping Station is also used to provide the extra impetus needed in the channel called the Counter Drain to keep water flowing through to the Tidal River.

The Counter Drain runs northward from Earith to Salter's Lode, parallel to the Middle Level Barrier Bank but outside the Ouse Washes flood area. Approximately 25,700 acres (10,400 ha) of Fenland are drained by a system of channels, ditches and pumping stations into the Counter Drain. Additionally, water flows in from 6,400 acres (2,600 hectares) of upland around Somersham. Under normal conditions, the power of gravity is sufficient for the Counter Drain to flow into the Tidal Ouse at Salter's Lode. When high tides prevent this, though, Welches Dam Pumping Station is used to lift flood water up and over the Middle Level Barrier Bank and into the Ouse Washes.

Two large pumping engines were installed at Welches Dam in 1948 and provided effective protection for many years. However, by 1998 the pumps had become unreliable (and had actually twice failed to operate properly). The problem was identified – the diesel engines that powered them were obsolete, and repair was proving increasingly difficult. A £250,000 project was undertaken to improve the situation. One of the slow (400-rpm) diesel engines was replaced by a high-speed (1,500-rpm) turbo-charged diesel engine. It was decided that the other engine was reliable enough to remain as a back-up, as it is only rarely necessary to run both engines at the same time. The original pump units were not replaced as they were found to be in good condition. Constant supervision of the pump was no longer necessary as the new engine was fully automated. A good deal of power is needed to move flood waters out of the river and on to the Washes storage reservoir, but the new facility is up to the task. The overall capacity of the station is now 12.6 cubic metres per second.

Nature Lends a Hand

There is one other component of the system that doesn't take much technical expertise to understand. Anyone cruising down one of the rivers or taking a walk along the banks, is bound to come across grazing sheep and cattle. What may not be obvious is that these animals are an important flood-defence mechanism – just as important as many of the sluices, barrier banks and pumps. Their grazing keeps the vegetation low; this helps to keep the rivers and channels clear, allowing the waters to flow freely and safely to the sea.

But this flood-defence mechanism is in danger. The first problem is that the last couple of decades have seen more floods taking place during the summer months, and hence less grazing of the land by cattle and sheep. The grazing lands are covered in a species of grass that is particularly favoured by the animals, but this grass only thrives when grazed and kept short. If increased flooding stops the cattle from grazing at times during the summer, their favourite grass will give way to a more dominant sweet red grass, *Glyceria*, which is unsuitable for grazing cattle – something of a vicious circle.

The second problem is that mixed farming is in decline, and many of today's farmers no longer keep cattle. The region is predominantly used for growing crops, and as more and more land is acquired by large conglomerates that focus on arable farming, this is increasingly the case. Also, whereas in the past many families kept a sheep or two, or a house cow, to supplement their provisions, this is now fairly rare. So, there are simply fewer animals being let out on to the land and the banks to graze. Compared with the engineering and financial challenges of multi-million pound sluices, hundreds of miles of embankments, pumping stations and all the rest, this might seem a trivial problem. It is not. Today, the Environment Agency, in its role of flood protector of the Fens, leases out grazing tenancies along many riverbanks. However, the many problems the British meat industry has experienced of late could mean there will be fewer graziers in the future. The alternative is mechanical mowing, a costly option which is not environmentally friendly.

II. Seeing the Past from the Present

There are plenty of places where one can find out more about the history of the Fens and see the past brought to life. The Wisbech Museum has an excellent collection that deals with many different aspects from drainage to consumerism to the abolition of slavery. If big machinery is your passion, the Prickwillow Drainage Museum is a great place to see painstakingly reconditioned diesel pumps, some in working condition.

There is a museum in Ely too, and it has a lot of interesting material to do with drainage, including a video of a BBC television programme from the late 1950s showing some of the last of the Fen Slodgers, Cambridge Camels (or whatever you choose to call the traditional Fenmen) demonstrating their eeling and trapping techniques – fascinating, and a real piece of social history. Also in Ely, the Cathedral is as splendid as its reputation. If you visit, just remember to look up. You'll see why.

Hermitage Hall in Downham Market is less well-known but absolutely packed with fascinating items of all sorts. The eclectic collection is full of photographs, as well as everything from clothing to cars to skates, household equipment, bicycles and parts of early airplanes. Well worth a visit, but be prepared to spend some time there – there is a great deal to see.

There are many excellent places where one can view the past from the present. This is a fairly comprehensive list, but is bound to miss some, so keep your eyes open.

Museums

(*Fens history and landscape*)
Ayscoughfee Hall Museum and Gardens
Churchgate
Spalding
Lincolnshire
01775 725468

(*Fen-edge village life*)
Burwell Museum
High Street
Burwell
Cambridgeshire
01638 605544

Chatteris Museum
14 Church Lane
Chatteris
Cambridgeshire
01354 696319

(*Cromwell family portraits and memorabilia*)
Cromwell Museum
High Street
Huntingdon
Cambridgeshire
01480 375830

Ely Museum
The Old Goal
Market Street
Ely
Cambridgeshire
01353 666655

(*Farming and village life*)
The Farmland Museum and Denny Abbey
Ely Road
Waterbeach
Cambridgeshire
01223 860988

March and District Museum
High Street
March
Cambridgeshire
01354 655300

(Fen skating memorabilia and archaeological relics)
The Norris Museum
The Broadway
St Ives
Cambridgeshire
01480 497314

(Commemorating a founder member of the National Trust)
Octavia Hill Birthplace Museum
1 South Brink Place
Wisbech
Cambridgeshire
01945 476358

Pinchbeck Engine and Land Drainage Museum
West Marsh Road
Pinchbeck
Spalding
Lincolnshire
01775 725468

Prickwillow Drainage Engine Museum
Off Queen Adelaide Road
Prickwillow
Ely
Cambridgeshire
01353 688360

The Stained Glass Museum
Ely Cathedral
The Chapter House
The College
Ely
Cambridgeshire
01353 660347

Whittlesey Museum
Town Hall
Market Street
Whittlesey
Cambridgeshire
01733 840968

Wisbech and Fenland Museum
Museum Square
Wisbech
Cambridgeshire
01945 583817

Churches

Crowland Abbey (partly ruined)
East Street
Crowland
Lincolnshire
01733 210499

Ely Cathedral
The Chapter House
The College
Ely
Cambridgeshire
01353 667735

Peterborough Cathedral
Peterborough
Cambridgeshire
01733 343342

Ramsey Abbey (ruins)
Abbey School
Ramsey
Cambridgeshire

Other Places of Interest

(*Restored and working windmill*)
Denver Windmill
Denver
Near Downham Market
Norfolk
01366 384009

(Re-created ancient fenland with archaeological park)
Flag Fen Bronze Age Excavations
The Droveway
Northey Road
Fengate
Peterborough
Cambridgeshire
0870 900 7798

(Fenland photos of the early twentieth century)
Lilian Ream Photographic Gallery
Tourist Information Centre
2-3 Bridge Street
Wisbech
Cambridgeshire
01954 583263

(Exhibitions and film)
Oliver Cromwell's House
29 St Mary's Street
Ely
Cambridgeshire
01353 662062

Tales of the Old Gaol House
Market Place
King's Lynn
Norfolk
01553 774297

III. Fenland Nature Reserves

Wicken Fen

This is the place to see the Fens as they used to be. Over 18 miles of trails will take you back to the landscape as it existed before drainage. At the right time of the year, the place swarms with butterflies and other insects, and there is plenty to interest the bird-watcher and plant enthusiast alike.

Wicken Village, nine miles south of Ely

The Wildfowl and Wetlands Trust Centre

One of the most famous wetland nature reserves in Britain. This is the winter home of the Bewick's and whooper swans, as well as a plethora of other birds, dragonflies and butterflies in their due seasons. Special events are staged on some winter evenings to see the thousands of swans by floodlight.

Near Welney Village, 12 miles north of Ely

Nene Washes RSPB Site

An excellent place to see wildfowl and waders.

Near Whittlesey

Lattersey Nature Reserve

28 acres of grasslands and ponds teeming with wildlife.

Whittlesey

Gault Wood

Particularly good for the tree enthusiast, with 10,000 newly planted trees, as well as lots of other flora and fauna to see.

March

Chettisham Meadows

Historic meadows covering 40 acres. One field is managed as a nature reserve.

Chettisham, near Ely

Soham Meadows

An area of grassland converted from arable fields. This is a designated SSSI (Site of Special Scientific Interest).

Soham, near Ely

Ouse Washes Nature Reserve

RSPB bird reserve.

Near Manea

IV. Glossary

Fenland was long a fairly isolated area and, inevitably, developed a distinctive dialect. Not surprisingly, Fenmen have many words describing watercourses, including:

cut   A man-made river or part of a river

drain   Not used in the normal sense – in the Fens this usually simply means a river, either natural or man-made

dyke   A man-made ditch

eau   From the French word for water, this usually refers to a man-made watercourse

lode   A ditch or small river – again, usually man-made

wash   Shortened form of 'washland' – land periodically flooded. In the Fens it refers specifically to the areas of land designed to act as flood storage reservoirs.

Words that are special or relevant to the Fens come from a number of sources including Anglo-Saxon, Danish, Dutch and French. Additionally, many Fen words have a Celtic origin. For example:

Fen word or phrase	Celtic equivalent
tiger (as in Fen Tiger)	In Welsh, the word 'tioga' means peasant
docky (the meal taken by workers in the fields)	docken or tocken = bread
seam	seim = grease

199

glaive (an eel-catching device)	glebe = sphere
Girvi or Gyrwe (ancient Celtic Tribe of the Fens)	could be derived from the Welsh words for charioteers or the runners, literally fleet of foot
Ely	helyg = willow (There are many willows around Ely where they were a valuable commodity.)

Place names have various origins amongst the many races who settled in the Fens:

- The word 'swidden' means a burnt clearing in Old English
- Also Old English, the suffix 'ing' means home of the followers of, for example, Dullingham (Dulla), Cottenham (Cotta), originally Cottingham, and Willingham (Wifel)
- The suffix 'ea' or 'ey' means island in both Old English and Norman and it can be seen that the towns and villages ending in this suffix are those that were higher than the undrained Fens (Ely, Manea, Ramsey, Stonea, Whittlesey, etc.)
- 'Pol', as in 'Walpole is the Old English word for pond
- Other Old English suffixes that can be found in the names of Fen villages and towns include 'toft' (homestead), 'by' (an adverbial participle of place meaning around, or about) and 'thorpe' (village).

Bibliography

Armstrong, Patrick, *The Changing Landscape* (Dalton, 1975)

Astbury, A.K., *The Black Fens* (Golden Hind Press, 1970)

Bloom, A., *The Fens* (Hale, 1953)

Bowers, P., *A Fenland Smallholding* (Crowood, 1986)

Ballcock, G., *Over My Boots* (Covent Garden Press, 1989)

Bevis, T., *Flooded Fens* (T. Bevis, 2001)

——, *A Guide to the Fens* (T. Bevis, 1966)

——, *A Journey Back in Time* (T. Bevis, 1976)

——, *Peterborough Past and Present* (T. Bevis, 1984)

——, *A Pocket Guide to the Fenland* (T. Bevis, 1990)

——, *Strangers in the Fens* (T. Bevis, 1983)

Charnley, P.R., *Old Dykes I Have Known* (Barny Books and P.R. Charnley, 1996)

Darby, H.C., *The Draining of the Fens* (Cambridge University Press, 1968)

——, *The Changing Fenland* (Cambridge University Press, 1983)

——, *The Medieval Fenland* (David & Charles, 1974)

Day, James Wentworth, *A History of the Fens* (Harrap, 1954)

——, 'Rum Owd Boys' (*East Anglian Magazine*, 1974)

Defoe, Daniel, *A Tour Through the Whole Island of Great Britain* (1724–6)

Doran, G., *The Great Ouse Flood Protection Scheme* (Dock and Harbour Authority, 1956)

Dorman, B.E., *The Story of Ely* (Black Horse, Norwich, 1986)

Dring, W.E., *The Fenland Story* (Cambridge and Isle of Ely Education Committee, 1967)

——, *Hereward's Isle* (Isle of Ely City Library, 1962)

Dugdale, Thomas, *England and Wales Delineated* (L. Tallis, 1850)

Ennion, E.A.R., *Adventurers' Fen* (Colt Books, 1996)

Fidler, K., *True Tales of Treasure* (Lutterworth, 1962)

Galloway, Bruce, *A History of Cambridgeshire* (Phillimore, 1983)

Godwin, Sir Harry, *Fenland: Its Ancient Past and Uncertain Future* (Cambridge University Press, 1978)

Gunning, Henry, ed. Winstanley, D.A., *Reminiscences of Cambridge: A Selection* (Cambridge University Publications, 1932)

Heathcote, J.M., *Reminiscences of Fen and Mere* (Longmans, Green, 1876)

Heathcote, J.M. and Tebbutt, C.G., *Skating* (Longmans Green, 1902)

Hills, R.L., *Machines, Mills and Uncountable Costly Necessities* (Goose, 1967)

Howat, Polly, *Ghosts and Legends of Lincs and The Fen Country* (Countryside Books, 1992)

Humphreys, John, *Hunter's Fen* (David & Charles, 1986)

Kingsley, Charles, *Prose Idylls* (MacMillan & Co., 1878)

Lord Orford's Voyage round the Fens in 1774, Introduction by H.J.K. Jenkins, Notes by Mary Liquorice (Cambridgeshire Libraries, 1987)

Lloyd, David W., *Historic Towns of East Anglia* (Gollancz/Peter Crawley, 1989)

Marlow, C., *Legends of the Fenland People* (Wakefield Publishing, 1976)

Marshall, S., *Fenland Chronicle* (Cambridge University Press, 1967)

Mee, A., *Cambridgeshire – The County of the Fens* (Hodder and Stoughton, 1965)

Miller, S.H. and Skertchly, S.B.J., *The Fenland: Past and Present* (Leach & Sons/Longman, 1878)

Parker, A.K., and Pye, D., *The Fenland* (David & Charles, 1976)

Pepys, Samuel, eds Latham, Robert and Matthews, William, *The Diary of Samuel Pepys* (Bell & Hyman, 1985)

Pryor, F., *English Heritage Flag Fen* (Batsford, 1991)

Ravensdale, Jack and Muir, Richard, *East Anglian Landscapes: Past and Present* (Joseph, 1984)

Ravensdale, J.R., *Liable to Floods* (Cambridge University Press, 1973)

Rindley, Keith, *Fenland Riots and the English Revolution* (Heinemann Educational Books, 1982)

Sheriff, R.C., *King John's Treasure* (Heinemann, 1954)

Stone, A., *Our Fenland Heritage* (1979)

Slater, John and Bunch, Allan, *Fen Speed Skating: An Illustrated History* (Cambridgeshire Libraries, 2000)

Storey, Edward, *Fen, Fire and Flood* (Cambridgeshire Libraries, 1986)

——, *Portrait of the Fen Country* (Hale, 1982)

——, *Spirit of the Fens*, (Hale, 1985)

——, *Call It A Summer Country* (Hale, 1978)

Summers, Dorothy, *The Great Level: A History of Drainage and Land Reclamation in the Fens* (David & Charles, 1976)

——, *The East Coast Floods* (David & Charles, 1978)

——, *The Great Ouse: The History of a River Navigation* (David & Charles, 1973)

Taylor, C., *The Cambridgeshire Landscape – Cambridgeshire and the Southern Fens* (Hodder and Stoughton, 1973)

Tebutt, C.F., *Hunts Folklore* (Friends of the Norris Museum, 1984)

Thirsk, J., *Fenland Farming in the 16th Century* (University College of Leicester, 1953)

West, W.W., *A Short and Concise History of the Fens* (Leach, 1800)

Young, Arthur, *Political Essays Concerning the Present State of the British Empire*, first published in 1772 (Clifton Books, 1970)

——, *General View of the Agriculture of the County of Norfolk*, first published in 1804 (Clifton Books, 1969)

Index